P9-DUT-859

11/18/80 グ乃

WITHDRAWN

JUN 24

DAVID O. McKAY LIBRARY
BYU-IDAHO

WITHDRAWN

DOYLE O. ____ LIBRARY
____ IDAHO

PLAYS
FOR THE
CHILDREN'S HOUR

by

CAROLYN SHERWIN BAILEY

An

AMERICAN CHILDHOOD
PRESENTATION

One Act Plays in Reprint

 Core Collection Books, inc.

GREAT NECK, NEW YORK

First Published 1931
Reprinted 1978

International Standard Book Number 0-8486-2032-1

Library of Congress — Catalog Card No. 77-094332

PRINTED IN THE UNITED STATES OF AMERICA

CONTENTS

THE MODERN CHILD IN FAIRYLAND

By Clare Tree Major *and*
Carolyn Sherwin Bailey

What is the birthright of the child today? Realism mainly. Yesterday's dreams are our everyday experiences. On his first rides, as soon as his eyes open to a recognition of anything, he is likely to find himself traveling in a car which speeds at a rate of fifty miles an hour apparently of its own volition. He looks above his head, and sees people flying about in the air. At home, he hears operas over the radio that are being sung a thousand miles away. If he wants to talk from New York to his father in Chicago, he lifts off the telephone receiver and does it. Light flows at the push of a button; darkness at the push of another. Everything that the child of fifty years ago thought of as an impossible marvel, the child of today sees as a logical accomplishment. He has no necessity for dreams, no opportunity for projecting himself into the future.

Compare the life of a child born on an American farm today with one of the same environment fifty years ago. The latter could read wonderful stories of quite impossible situations and climax, but which aroused his imagination because they carried him so far afield from his everyday experiences. He fancied the possibility of flight through the air, of the sound of voices and music from an unseen source, of locomotion and transportation without horses, of the possibility of human communication across seas. All these situations were so absolutely impossible to the child of the last generation that their very aloofness brought them close to him. They drew his mind into the wonder world of the imagination which gave him an opportunity to vision what the world would be if such miracles were truth. He loved to hear and read stories of adventure and romance in the impossible, things the imagination held.

Children born into this generation are handicapped so far as impulse for constructive imagination is concerned. Educators do not sufficiently realize this. There is a dearth of the stuff of dreams with which they can enfold their lives. The magic carpet is replaced by the aeroplane; Aladdin's lamp by the spotlight of the motion picture which gives children a false idea of the drama and whose whole mode stunts the imagination.

The present emphasis in education is upon reality. We believe that we are the only living beings in the world, and because science has brought hitherto unseen phenomenon to our everyday lives in actuality we feel that we have reached the limit of understanding and vision. We are open to nothing; therefore the children whom we influence become restricted in their thinking. In nothing are we so stupid as in our surety that every external vision marks the limit of human sight, sound and touch. We draw a hard, fast line and on one side of it we place ourselves saying, this is real, and this is unreal. A Hindu magician performs before our eyes an astounding feat of magic; we immediately set ourselves about the unnecessary task of proving his skill a trick. A child lost in the beauty and heavenly unreality of the forest tells us that he saw a wood sprite, or that for an hour he played and talked with a fairy; we proceed to deny this truth of childhood. Children see more than adults. We are as blind today in our outlook on the fairy world as were the people of Columbus' time who knew that the earth was flat.

Children are vastly more truthful than we. The child imagination is characterized by a fluidity whereas we are enclosed within a shell of our own building. They live for a brief matchless period in the Unseen from which they have so lately come to us. Childhood mirrors clearly everything that is real; this is proved in our relations with these little ones before their spirits are hurt by fear and dread, and the well-springs of their spontaneity are choked by the dam of adult reasoning. May we not then ask ourselves if the child sees something in fairy lore which we do not? Should we not make more constructive use of the drama in education than we have heretofore?

The dramatic instinct of childhood should be fostered and given expression through the school-room production of fairy plays. Do not feel that the imagination is an inward turning activity of the mind. It is the root of all action. Much reading and listening to fairy stories forces a child back into a life of fantasy which in time becomes subconscious and repressive. But the development of school drama in which the story of imaginative appeal is interpreted in a simple, forceful way in activity has a useful reaction upon every phase of life. The best example of this is the production of that ancient and most beautiful nature allegory, "The Sleeping Beauty." The story is well-known and a favorite with all children. Tell them that every tree bud, ugly bulb, dark root and sleeping seed bursting its apparent death sleep of the winter expresses the truth told in the story. Its meaning is that of the awakening miracle of a green and flowering earth at the touch of the sun, as the princess is roused to life by the kiss of the prince. The best acting version of the play is the arrangement by Theodora Du Bois, but better still will be the children's dramatization told in their own realistic dialogue.

The simple and beautiful stage setting which we have designed and used in The Children's Theater for our production of "The Sleeping Beauty" could be copied with little effort and great charm in any schoolroom. The background is the same for all the scenes. We use a long, fulled backdrop of white cheesecloth, gathered quite closely so as to make deep folds, and this is hung at the back of the room or stage from the top to the bottom of the space. At one side of this is a red light and at the opposite side a blue light which, thrown upon the folds of the background and caught in them, makes a truly beautiful effect as of shimmering silk for the back of the throne room. For the first scene, that of the christening party of the baby princess, a draped chair wide enough for the throne stands at the back center. In front is a plain wood box trimmed with ruffles of white crepe paper and streamers of the same for the cradle of the princess. This cradle stands upon a stool or a high chair without a back. The king and queen are seated upon the throne, and the three fairies who give the princess their good gifts of a golden apple for grace, a mirror for beauty, and a golden plate for riches are grouped about the cradle. The bad fairy who gives a needle with which the little princess will prick herself and fall into her sleep of a hundred years enters at the end of this scene.

The costuming should be as simple as the stage setting. The fairies are dressed alike in white cheesecloth. Gold and silver radiator paint is splashed over the costumes of two giving a realistic effect of the characters they represent. The third fairy is dressed in crystal. The cheesecloth making her dress is coated lightly with glue and then scattered with the frost powder which is used now at the holiday season. The dress is trimmed with the sparkling artificial icicles used for Christmas trees. The bad fairy wears a dress of black. The queen's costume may be modeled on medieval lines, close fitting and with long, flowing sleeves. It is made of some soft fabric in warm crimson. Cotton poplin dyed or painted with dye colors is lovely in stage craft for children. In these costumes avoid a stiff unwielding textile as sateen or cambric. Unbleached muslin drapes well and takes color satisfactorily. This may be used for the king's robes. Trim this with the woolen side of canton flannel stitched at intervals with black, or painted with black dots. Avoid the use of cotton batting as ermine. It is not easily handled by children and not so effective as flannel. The dress of the princess as she appears when grown is made on the same lines as her mother's, of unbleached canton flannel, the soft side out. Both the princess and the queen may have loose wide girdles of gilded stuffs upon which are sewed the bright artificial jewels used by dressmakers in embroidery. The prince wears a smocked jerkin and trunks, if the latter are available. Underwear may be dyed and used in place of the trunks, and a smock made of unbleached muslin. If this muslin is stenciled in purple before the garment is cut, and the design filled in back of the stenciling with gold, a beautiful effect of brocade is obtained.

The throne has any desired draping, a velvet curtain of purple or blue, a Spanish shawl, a Persian rug. In the last scene of the play in which the castle sleeps, the princess is seen asleep upon the throne. The king and queen sleep also at her right and left, their backs to the throne, and the various attendants are grouped about the stage. It is not possible to tell you the beauty of this stage setting with the radiance of the red and blue lights thrown from the sides of the background. The costuming I have described has been selected and designed in our theater for beauty and its lighting possibilities. The result is artistic and has a quality of irridescence which is essential for such a play as "The Sleeping Beauty."

It may be desirable to plan an additional scene showing the forest through which the prince wanders in his search for the princess. This stage setting also, as we have designed it, may be copied by children in the average schoolroom with beautiful result. One method of making a woodland set is particularly adaptable for the craftwork of young children. We cut two or three strips, two or three feet in width, from heavy black mosquito netting. These strips hang from ceiling to floor of the stage and are tacked in place. Cut trunks, branches and leaves of trees from brown and green paper and paste on the netting to imitate forest trees. The effect is lovely.

We have designed also a silhouette setting for a woods scene of equal simplicity. It has possibilities of much beauty when lighting is used in the production of the play. Drop a length of mosquito netting down one side of the room near the wall and paste upon it brown paper cut to look like the trunks of trees. From gray muslin or canton flannel make a curtain to stretch across the entire front of the space where the action is to take place and extending as low as would the foliage of forest trees. This curtain is slashed, cut in holes, in slits, and the edge made ragged as are the spaces and shadows of a wood. Light thrown through this curtain from the back gives the effect of an enchanted forest in front of which the players appear. The entire action of a woodland scene should take place in front of this curtain, with no other lighting.

The great educational value to children of producing the plays for themselves is recognized I think by every teacher; and by education I mean the development and control of thought and emotion as well as a sense of mental, emotional and physical co-ordination. I wonder if teachers or parents—I should say parents because I believe they are much less alive to this than are teachers—realize that much harm may be done as well as good. My experience in the theater leads me to condemn the point of view which makes of what should be to the child a great game of pretend a most harmful exhibition of vanity and over-stimulation. When plays are given, the audience should be the least significant thing. The finished nature of the final performance should not be emphasized as a responsibility to the child. Free expression should be the result aimed at, but public performances frequently have the opposite result, a painful inhibition through fear of imperfection.

The teacher must visualize the aims of education before she can successfully teach a class of children. More than this, she should be able to mentally see a child's point of view in order to completely understand him. The man in the complicated maze of business relations today uses imagination in visioning and bringing about success. The artist must have visualized his picture before he touches his canvas. The little child, whose perceptive faculties are sharply acute for gathering thought material and from these small prismatic bits of life making a pattern for his own ideals and behavior, must use these faculties. Since human life and development are impossible without the most active use of the imagination, something must supply the modern child with the stimulus to vision which the perfection of modern mechanism has destroyed. To my mind nothing is left for this but the fairy and folk tale. Transmutation, an organic change from one form or substance to another, in any of the three kingdoms is still an impossibility. Transmutation is one of the elemental ideas on which fairy tales are built. Neither chemical investigation nor the perfection of the microscope or the telescope have succeeded in revealing to mortal vision the secrets of the little people of the woods and the sea, the mountains and the underground. Sometimes these delectable creatures reveal themselves to the child's undoubting gaze. But for the child not so favored, the fairy play and the theater can supply something of his need. For assuredly never more than today have children needed the wonder of fairy contact.

IN THE SCHOOLROOM THEATER

By CLARE TREE MAJOR *and*
CAROLYN SHERWIN BAILEY

The elementary schoolroom equipped with movable tables and chairs offers opportunity for staging child dramatizations with unusual effect. The modern proscenium is no longer constructed on one plane. The acting space of the theater today is being enlarged to include two, three, and perhaps four different levels, one above another. This has the result of bringing the audience closely within the action of the play, and giving a more intimate opportunity to follow the action on various changing levels of vision and imagination. It is even possible that spaces back and above the stage may be filled by the persons of the chorus or suggest the presence of invisible players, in this manner stimulating the illusion and bringing about a closer contact between the actors and those who look on.

A recently built proscenium for staging a fairy play in a children's theater in New York well illustrates this plan. The setting was constructed for producing the play on three distinct planes, as if the action were taking place on a series of broad steps. The first level, built only slightly higher than the level of the children in the audience, represented the dungeon of a palace with its dark foreground, barred door, and stone wall. Next above this, on a second level, was a slightly higher platform carpeted with green to represent a garden and showing the palace in which the princess of the fairy

11

tale lived. When it became necessary for the action
to be transferred from the level of the palace to that of
the dungeon, the characters climbed down by
means of a ladder, or were let down by a rope.
The background of the castle was represented by
means of a series of painted panels showing trees, a
meadow and sheep at the back of the castle. Just
above this, constructed upon the castle roof, was
the level of the forest. A mossy covering with
trees was placed directly over the castle, narrow
of course, but allowing for action when the scene
was transferred to the woods. The background
for the entire set was a gorgeously colored curtain
in black and gold painted in a design of old-world
tapestry which gave the atmosphere of the period
to the play. It will be readily seen that such an
arrangement of proscenium as this allows for the
entire action of the play without change of stage
setting and delay between acts. It has also the
unusual effect of harmony and permanence in the
entire production not possible when the sets are
changed for the different acts. The whole proscenium
in this case was enclosed in a decorative frame of
white cloth with a pattern of gold scroll work as
if it were the framework of a picture.

I realize that such a proscenium may seem impossible to reproduce in the schoolroom, but it is not
nearly so difficult to build as it sounds. It is pecu-
liarly adapted to the "activity room" of a school.
Everything save the chairs is removed, these being
grouped for the audience in the middle and back
of the room. The lower level of the stage is built
of wooden boxes nailed together. The second level
may be constructed of small strong tables, all of the
same size and placed securely on top of the boxes.

These two levels are covered with rugs of the kind and color needed. A painted curtain covering the space at the back will complete the illusion. It would probably not be possible to arrange for three levels in this schoolroom stage, but in producing simple fairy and folk plays with young children, why not arrange to have part of the action take place on the plane of·the audience? A space like an aisle may be reserved between the chairs in the center of the room where those children who are not principals in the play may interpret their parts. Wood nymphs, brownies, animals, elves, in fact all those loved characters of childhood who make up the chorus of the play, belong for their entrance and exit here among the spectators, and in being so placed save acting space on the stage. This arrangement allows the audience to become a living part of the drama.

The teacher who must stage her play in a schoolroom of the older type in which the desks and seats are fastened to the floor need not be discouraged. She has a wide space at the front reserved for class activities which is quite adequate for arranging an interesting and imaginative setting without resorting to the trouble of building a stage.

The floor space reserved in the front of the room for the stage should be covered to create the needed ground plan for the play. A forest or market place demands a green rug, or one of brown. In the open months of the year real leaves, moss and leafy boughs may be spread upon the floor of the stage. Evergreens may cover the floor for the staging of the Christmas play. If the play demands an indoor set, rag rugs, floor coverings from the children's homes, straw matting or linoleum will serve to cover the space where the action is to take place. The most important consideration in staging the schoolroom play is to plan a set which will create an effect of illusion. It has been found that very simple scenery and properties constructed by the children themselves will best create the necessary effect of fantasy for a dramatization.

Schoolroom handicraft may be utilized for transforming the stage into an outdoor scene. Dye several yards of ordinary unbleached muslin a soft green. There should be enough of this muslin to stretch across the stage. When it has dried in the desired color, fringe it in various lengths and ragged outlines and also slit and cut it throughout in holes so that the whole piece is tattered, letting the light through as the leafy outlines of a forest allow the light and shadow to show. Stretch this green cloth across the room either back of the stage, or near enough to the front so that the players may interpret their action directly underneath it. A local contractor will surely be willing to contribute enough light board or what is known as sheet rock to use for outlined tree trunks which stand at either side of this green fringed curtain. These tree trunks should be painted in spots of brown and green to imitate dappled woods shadows, and they are placed just back of the curtain. This easily made woods set is picturesque in its simplicity for the schoolroom. It is also very practical as the trees at either side of the stage allow for the entrance and exit of the cast.

This fringed curtain may be the foreground and screening for improvised scenery placed at the back of the stage. A few chairs arranged in a square and covered with a draping of cloth make a house. The same chairs having broomsticks tied to their backs and covered with muslin painted gray outside and black on the inside, make a cave for trolls, elves, or gnomes. If the muslin is painted in browns, reds, yellow and orange before it is fringed and cut in holes, we have a representation of the autumn woods. Painted in blues and greens, it may be used as the entrance to a cave at the bottom of the sea from which mermaids emerge. You can readily see how this simple curtaining device may be used in the staging of such plays of childhood as "Hansel and Gretel," with the gingerbread house of the witch in the background; scenes from "Hiawatha," broomsticks being used as the foundation for a tepee with real shocks of corn about the stage; and the escapades of the child's beloved brownies who live and play within the safe precincts of the forest.

A schoolroom set for the play which needs interiors for its action is quite as simple to construct. Here again cheap unbleached muslin is the material used for the background and scenery. The furnishings of a room, including chairs, a table, candlestick, pictures, a mirror, door, and windows, can be roughly sketched on this muslin and painted. This backdrop is stretched and tacked to the wall at the back of the stage. Paint two lengths of the muslin with dyes, using a pale color at the top and shading the design until it is quite dark at the bottom. Hang these long drapes at the side of the stage thus creating a false proscenium and making possible the concealing of the actors. If these side curtains can be hung by means of curtain rings to wires stretched across the room, they may be used as a curtain.

The adaptability of unbleached muslin for school-room staging of plays is unlimited. It may be painted on both sides for an interior set, hung at the back of the stage by means of curtain rings on hooks in the wall and turned when another background is desired. Thus we have a painted picture of Cinderella's kitchen on one side of our background and on the other the wall of the palace throne room. We may paint a nursery scene on one side, and a garden on the other. This garden scene is particularly effective with a design of huge green leaves and vivid flowers which even the youngest children can outline and color with almost no help. An effect of flowers makes a charming curtain for the front of a stage if it is possible to hang the patterned fabric from the ceiling.

The arts and crafts encouraged and taught in preparing for the schoolroom play are indeed educational. The children should be stimulated to make as many of the properties required by the play as possible; caps for elves, brownies and gnomes, wands twined and trimmed for king and queen, fairies, and jesters, the colored leaves which cover the stage for the autumn play, and the various accessories carried by the actors. We find that a framework of rather fine wire can be shaped, covered with muslin, and then painted to represent such "props" as the turtle in "Alice in Wonderland," the ravens in Hans Christian Andersen's "Snow Queen," and various other objects which are essential to the story but which should be light enough not to hamper the actors.

The A. B. C. of stage action, those rules which every actor must learn to obey until they become habits in order to keep the harmony and rhythm of the dramatic picture, may be learned by children and applied in their dramatic play for grace and unconsciousness. Explain the reasons for these rules of action; because the play is a picture, a very beautiful picture, these are not arbitrary commands, but opportunities for preserving the composition of the scene and helping the audience to enter more completely into the spirit of the play. The important rules of acting are these:

The characters in the play should never stand in a straight row. They may be grouped in twos and threes for the dialogue as the dramatization demands this, but the straight line formation is not beautiful and it also has the effect of spoiling the lines and contours established by the scenery.

All movement on the stage should be simple. The maximum of effect must be accomplished through the medium of effort. Suppose we have Cinderella seated in a chair in front of the hearth, and her fairy godmother appears at a door at the right. Cinderella rises and passes out without going behind her chair, thus facing the audience until she has made her exit. This rule applies unfailingly. Economize motion on the stage, and move about so as to preserve the picture. This means passing in front of, not behind, other actors, and in front of furniture, trees, and shrubbery. Should there be three people in a group at the right up-stage, and the player at the right wishes to speak to the one at the left, he steps a little in front and leans toward the left. If the player in the center wishes to speak to the one on his right or left, he steps a little forward.

The interest of the players must be centered on the action, and always on the moment of action. We will say that the child Hiawatha is calling the birds and little animals of the forest to him. The players keep their eyes on him. They reflect in facial expression and gesture his eagerness, watch his movements, share his longing and his joy when the little wild brothers of the woods seem to come at his call. Unfailingly the players must co-operate to make the picture of the play a unit of action. They are interested, shocked, sad, merry, curious with the principals. Children do this unconsciously in their free play; they excel in such mimicry. The part of the teacher is only to foster their instinctive dramatic feeling.

There are some minor rules of action which will help with the success of the schoolroom play. The actor never stands or walks with his feet turned outward; the feet should be almost parallel and one slightly in front of the other. Feet turned out tend to foreshorten the body and make the player look grotesque, and out of proportion. The feet should never be crossed. This shortens the costume. Two players should never stand or seat themselves at exactly the same moment; such action is ludicrous from the point of view of the audience. You will remember how this point is illustrated in the action of Tweedledum and Tweedledee in "Alice in Wonderland"; it results in comedy.

Where the costuming of the play calls for dress to which the children are unused, see that they have a chance to wear and rehearse in it enough so that they will not be uncomfortable. Everything about the costume for the schoolroom play should be as natural as possible to obviate self-consciousness. If the little folks have an opportunity to wear trains, coifs, wigs, and long skirts beforehand, they will quite naturally develop the short steps, the dignity, and the manners these clothes demand. The curtain call of today requires that the same scene be preserved upon which the curtain fell. If there is a call for players who were not in this scene, they are placed in as nearly as possible the same position as they had in their last appearance.

The play of the present should express two qualities,—truth and beauty. These are inherent in normal, happy childhood, and should be the main object in staging child plays in the schoolroom.

MASKS AND WIGS IN SCHOOLROOM DRAMATICS

By FRANK M. RICH

The outstanding difficulty in the way of immediate adoption of the project method in all school subjects is the trouble of finding desirable pieces of work that will enlist the heartiest enthusiasm of youngsters, and square with the usual scholastic requirements. One of the most promising projects for children of any age, on the playground or at school, is the designing and use of homemade masks and make-ups. From the standpoint of motivation, masking makes its own strong appeal to the natural instincts of childhood. Everybody with youth in his veins finds it exhilarating to escape from the confines of drab reality, and enter into the dramatic world of fancy and romance. Masking leads to dramatization and that to a generous amount of reading, literature, language, music, art and, with it all, good-fellowship. It provides classes with live social situations wherein character development through group action, leadership, initiative, mutual consideration, assistance and the like come in for practice along with the three R's. Above all, there is wholesome contact with reality, opportunity to test opinions, impulses, abilities and, by trial and success, to build up a foundation of mental stamina and common sense. Since the materials for wigs, masks and properties as we make them cost next to nothing, here is a field where we can afford to let pupils plan and execute in their own way and learn through experience. The final outcome of the activity can be made much broader than one evening's mummery. It can be applied to all sorts of occasions, from a back-yard circus to a historical pageant.

Quite convincing make-ups are possible with only ordinary clothing for a foundation. For example, rows of ice-cream spoons, sewed down the front of an old coat, in imitation of military buttons and buttonholes, make a striking band uniform. The cheap tin washers used for nailing building paper, if punched and sewed to a shirt or sweater, make a realistic suit of armor. The same washers serve for gypsy bangles or buttons for a uniform. Hollow squares of white cardboard, fastened to the knees or over the instep with a band of old inner tire, will equip a regiment with silver buckles for colonial make-up. Gather up some side draperies of odd material on any sort of skirt, and out flounces a realistic Martha Washington. Ruffs, scarfs and the like cover a multitude of omissions. Usually specially cut and tailored garments will not be missed, for the most distinctive part of a make-up is not the clothing or shoes, but the head covering, wig, beard or mask, with perhaps a characteristic accessory. Thus a crown and scepter mark a king or queen; a three-cornered hat, wig, epaulettes and sword, a colonial soldier; a tall hat, collar, buckles and gun, a Puritan; and so on. All such articles of make-up, from a finger ring to an elephant, can be made from old cord, paper and paste, with no expense, except possibly for the dye, paint or crayons used to color them.

A variety of wigs, colonial, western, Indian, grandmother, braided and curled, can be made by

completely untwisting the coarse hemp cord used
for tying express packages, separating the fibers
neatly into small strands, eight or ten strands to
the inch when tied, and fastening them together
in a broad flat band by tying the strands side by
side with a double cord of strong, waxed thread;
or tight double twists of soft, fine wire, such as
window screens are made from, may be used for
tying. The band of fiber will need to be about
ten inches long, or long enough to reach from the
top of the forehead to the occiput. The wig is
placed on the head of the wearer with a seam of
thread or wire forming the part in the hair over
the middle of the head. The fiber can be smoothed
down to fit the head and then braided or coiled in
keeping with the character.

For men's colonial wigs, two or three extra
curls can be added at the side with good effect.
Wind a few strands of fiber around a pencil. Put
some thread or long fiber into a needle and weave
it back and forth a few times the length of the
roll, to keep the roll together. Then dip it into
boiling water or steam it in the mouth of a teakettle
to set the curl permanently. Stitch the curls to
the wig in a single, double or triple row at the
temples. For ladies' colonial wigs, add two or
three such curls of varying length to hang from
behind one ear down to the bosom. For curls or a
Dutch-cut it will be necessary to weave in a few
strands of thread or fiber around the head to keep
the wig on. This is best done on the head of the
wearer.

For many effects, the natural white or yellow
hemp will answer without coloring. Natural yellow can be turned to an iron gray by dipping it in a

solution of laundry blueing or writing ink before wig is made.   Other colors can be obtained with the cotton dyes sold everywhere.   The commonest colors will be black and various intensities of seal brown. For "red" hair use light brown, and for the comic "carroty red" use orange.

When children are to make up as adults, eyebrows of the same color as the hair always lend a convincing touch.   Actors use spirit gum to fasten eyebrows, moustache and side whiskers to the face, but as this is expensive and hard to remove, it is preferable for the amateur to use an adhesive wax made by melting together equal parts of resin and beeswax, with a very little lard or olive oil to soften it.   Since a large proportion of oil and resin makes flypaper, the reason for sparing the soft ingredient is evident.   This wax holds a wisp of hair of any size securely, but allows it to be removed at will. The same wax can be used for coating the thread used for making wigs and beards.

Full beards are made on a fairly stiff piece of soft iron wire bent from under the mouth, across the cheeks and around the back of the ears, to hold on like spectacles.   If a moustache is needed, a short piece of wire is added under the nose.   The fiber, rather shorter and finer than for wigs, is sewed to the wire with waxed thread, using a coarse buttonhole stitch.   If the beard is untrimmed, longer fibers should be used for the upper lip, center chin and upper cheek than for the side of the chin and adjoining part of the cheek.

Masks, hats, armor, statuary and all sorts of utensils, from a feather pen to a cookstove, can be made from the cheap, ready-to-hand materials, discarded news- and wrapping-paper, string and paste, with sometimes a little wood, old wire or screen for the framework of the larger pieces.

Probably the commonest call is for hats and grotesque human or animal masks. Wet a double handful of flour with a cupful of cold water. Stir thoroughly to remove all lumps and leave a smooth batter. While stirring constantly, add gradually one and a half quarts of boiling water. Stirring and slow mixing is the secret of smoothness. Cook for a few minutes, preferably in a double boiler, as the flour mixture is very likely to stick to the bottom and burn. As it cooks enough, the flour changes from an opaque white to translucent. While the paste is cooling, make the inside core of the object you wish to model around a ball of crushed dry newspaper. Wrap on one sheet after another, until the ball is approximately the right size and shape. String tied round in various directions will hold the ball together. As it approaches completion, dampen the paper with water, so that the outside layers will press down smoothly and take shape better than dry paper can be made to do. The final touches, such as noses, lips, brows and all protusions, can be put on with paper thoroughly wet.

The outside covering, the hat or mask itself, is made of tough kraft paper, torn into long strips, dipped into the paste and stuck on, one at a time, smoothly and in various directions till a layer several thicknesses deep completely covers the article. If the kraft paper used varies in thickness, put large, coarse pieces on first, and small, thin pieces on last, so as to cover all folds and wrinkles and leave the outside surface perfectly smooth. Torn edges are better than cut edges, as they stick down tightly and are invisible.

Kraft paper is surprisingly tough and durable and these masks will stand considerable use, but if unusual strength and wear are desired, the outside can be covered with knitted goods, soaked in paste and spread out smoothly. If the article is to be colored with anything that mixes with water, ink, dye, water colors, calcimine or colored blackboard crayons sized with a little glue, it will save time to put the foundation coat on while the article is still wet. For crayolas, gilding or oil paints, the surface will need to be done dry, also for the fine touches used in finishing the painting.

When the mask is molded it will need to be dried quickly by putting it on the top of the heater or furnace or in an open oven, where the water can evaporate rapidly without danger of scorching. When the outside is hard and dry, the shell is cut open with a sharp knife and the newspaper core removed. For solid objects, of course, this last step is unnecessary.

If a number of hollow articles of the same size and shape are needed, such as hats, breastplates and masks, they can be molded, one at a time, on a matrix of the right shape made of paper as described. When dry, the outside is greased with tallow, covered with a lining layer of wet newspaper, followed by the usual kraft paper and paste. When hard, the first article can be slipped off and a second molded on the same foundation.

All sorts of properties—andirons, candlesticks, kettles, jugs, shields, spears, trumpets, miniature models and so on—can be made by the one process. A fine sword and scabbard of any particular pattern can be made on a wire foundation. Grease the blade with tallow and make the scabbard of pasted kraft paper.

The jolliest of make-ups are the animals, horses, elephants, chimpanzees and folk-tale beasts. The head is a mask, made as I have described. The body is a suit of gray or brown cloth made like a child's sleeping garment, with a blanket sewed to the head and spread over the back in the case of a horse or elephant. A special favorite among the animal make-ups is the pony and rider combination played by one person. Make a frame of rather heavy wire; iron telephone wire, or the wire that sometimes comes around barrel hoops and boxes is good. The center of the frame is the saddle, an elliptical loop of wire of such a size that it can be drawn up over the hips and then given a quarter turn; it holds itself in place on the wearer by pressing against the sides of his waist. This saddle is attached by radial strips of wire to another larger ellipse or oval which outlines the body of the horse. The radial wires should be curved like the horse's back, the rear one twisted into a loop for attaching the tail of raveled rope.

The head consists of a loop of wire shaped like the front view of a horse's face, including the ears. Another wire reaches from the top of the head to the bottom of the chin, and is shaped like the side view of the horse's face, with the open mouth. The first loop can be bent somewhat to complete the side view of the face and give fullness to the muscles of the jaw. The head is fastened to the body with three wires forming the neck, two at the back of the neck continued to form the shoulders, and one at the throat. The contour of these neck pieces will depend upon the style of steed—rather straight for "Spark Plug," and curved for a spirited charger.

Fill the inside of the head and neck with crushed newspaper and cover all with pasted kraft paper, kiln-dried as described. Cover the body with a trailing cloth that extends to the ground and covers the wearer's legs. False legs hung from the rider's waist outside the horse's blanket create the illusion of a midget on horseback.

One difficulty connected with work with paste at home or at school is that it is rather messy. Workers will need to dress in old togs and protect themselves with overalls and aprons. Floors and furniture will need to be protected with a generous layer of paper. Even then, considerable scrubbing up will be needed when it is all over. Fortunately, paste is not hard to remove from either furniture or clothing. What constitutes a serious objection against the work to one instructor, the tendency to messiness and disorder, will be considered a real advantage to another. It offers an opportunity to teach the value of care and foresight in the only way they can be taught, by practical experience. How can tendencies to blundering heedlessness be discouraged and habits of neatness established better than in the natural outcomes of work that permits a choice between two ways of doing things?

IN THE PLAYGROUND THEATER

By Clare Tree Major *and*
Carolyn Sherwin Bailey

The development of the play and pageant for children in the open is not dependent upon the outdoor theater. Every school has either a space in front of the building which can be used, or there is an adjacent playground or community play field which may be adapted for the staging of those plays which are not only of interest to boys and girls but lend themselves by their dramatic content to the free interpretation which is possible only in a natural setting.

The first problem of staging the outdoor play for children is that of the site and the best arrangement of seats for the audience in relation to the location or natural setting which is to be used for the stage. Let us consider a bare school playground without grass or trees, as it exists in many towns, limited in space, with perhaps a wood or iron fence surrounding it, but nothing of growing beauty about which to build a setting. Here we have a most interesting problem in stagecraft which may be solved for real artistry and used as a basis for the pageant which is so delightful to childhood. The audience in this case is placed facing the school, the facade of the school being used for a background. Many of our public-school buildings, especially the large, new consolidated schools of the rural sections, have classic architectural effects in entrances, doorways, and pillars which could not be duplicated in scenic effect. If we use the front of the school as our back drop, there is the added advantage of having a convenient means of entrance and exit. Frequently there is a winding path from the back around one side of the building which makes an ideal entrance for the child pageant or the chorus of the play, the principal players using the school doorway for their entrance.

This plan for the outdoor theater, in which the building facade is the background, allows for the staging of many modern dramas of childhood, and the historical play which demands a colonial or classic type of architecture in its scenes. But we should never make use of the school building in this way without in some way disguising it. The element of the imagination must enter always into the child's play. The doorway may be twined with vines and flowering boughs to represent a summer cottage, or draped with flags for the patriotic or historical pageant. Place the audience so that the facade is seen from an unusual angle, the door at one side, and transform the path by means of a temporary hedge made also of boughs. Or the path may be disguised as a garden gate over which flowers twine, and in this case we use it for a side entrance. The steps of the schoolhouse entrance lend themselves to the grouping of the players in a tableau, and frequently this doorway is wide enough to allow for some of the acting taking place upon the steps. In the event that the steps are too narrow erect a temporary roofless porch for a stage so that the players may be slightly raised from the level of the children who are the spectators.

The audience of this school-yard theater should be placed at the farthest possible point compatible with clear vision and hearing so that the element of illusion may be preserved. The individual acting takes place on the steps and the mass formation below, on the ground, if it is not possible to build the temporary stage. Really lovely effects are possible with this arrangement if the teacher and children put all their effort into preserving and emphasizing those lines in the building facade which are essential for the spirit of the play, but disguise the rest of the background with greenery or bunting. It is surprising how perfectly the illusion of the play may be thus obtained where, without the school building, it could not be staged except with elaborate scenery which children could neither build or shift.

Our second problem in outdoor stagecraft is the playground space of possibly one-half an acre, bare, and fenced with ugly pickets or otherwise barren in possibility of beautifying. This is a fertile spot for developing the outdoor drama because, with all its bareness, it is dedicated to the spirit of play of the town's children. The only way if differs from the school-yard theater is in its lack of a suitable building for a background. We will assume that this loss is an asset rather than a liability, since it suggests the producing of the fantastic play, or those of the Shakespearean dramas, which can be adapted for children. We seat our audience here with the thought of reserving the most suitable screening space which they will face. Usually the playground fence offers the only possible foundation for the background, and this we proceed to build up with either lathes or light poles until it is high enough for a back drop. This foundation is covered as thickly as possible with green boughs, and if flowering shrubs are available, these will be truly beautiful for such screening of the characters in the play. On either side of this natural back drop there should be a group of shrubbery about ten feet in height, and these green spots are spaced thirty feet apart. The shrubs are placed slightly in front of the greenery at the back so as to allow for the entrance and exits of the players, or as sets for the grouping of a chorus or the mass formation used in the action of the play. The utility and freedom of this arrangement will be readily seen. It allows for an acting space which gives the illusion of a stage to the audience, and provides opportunity for almost any action called for in the play.

We will suppose, as our third problem in staging the outdoor play, that there is nothing at all of value for scenery in the available space, not a tree, a wall, or an ornamental doorway. We have nothing upon which to build the play save the children's dramatic instinct, and a small allotment of earth with the sky overhead. This is frequently the case when there is a large community playground in your town divided into spaces for different recreation interests and with scattered playground apparatus which cannot be moved. The outdoor players in this field have only a corner set apart for their activities. Let us utilize this corner for dramatic illusion and beauty. This is achieved by closely imitating nature. We must consider how this portion of ground would have looked if it had not been cleared of its growing things; very likely it was a hollowed bowl with a bit of the woods back of it. Very possibly it was colored with wild flowers. We shall proceed to restore it to its old heritage of spring and summer.

The audience is placed, as in the bowl of an outdoor playhouse, in a semicircle. We build a light lattice screen of thin strips of wood or, better still, several of these screens, to be set up wherever they are needed. Green boughs are twined thickly through the lattices, or they are covered with greenery made of crepe paper. The latter plan will be found very satisfactory, as the children themselves will be able to make the paper leaves and vines, and the screens will be lighter and more easily moved than when they are covered with branches. Crepe paper flowers may be made for such lattice screening; wisteria for the Japanese play, or cherry blossoms, roses, apple blossoms, and poppies for the garden play.

These three simple arrangements of a natural setting for the child's outdoor dramatic interpretations will be found to cover almost any school or playground situation. The rural school is able to arrange for a grassy bowl on the edge of a woods, or stage its play in a garden where trees or a hedge form a natural back drop, but in any case masses of fresh green should be placed at the right and left to allow for the essential action and further disguise the setting for its effect of transformation.

The truly important consideration of the outdoor theater, particularly for children, is the harmonious relation of the audience to the players. We should not scatter or spread the action of the play over too great spaces, as such a plan tends not only to blur the effect of color, but makes it impossible for the audience to focus in attention. This matter solves itself if we select the best screening plan for the stage, not too widely spaced, and with as much depth of green as we can bank. The diction of the players should be specially taught for the outdoor play. Teach your child actors to avoid raising the pitch of their voices. A low voice carries farthest in the open. There is always a tendency among children to be shrill outdoors. This must be corrected. The enunciation must be particularly clear; each word should be a unit of enunciation or the dialogue will be confused.

Costuming for the outdoor play is quite different from that for the schoolroom theater, because of the influence upon fabrics and colors of the natural surroundings. A general rule would be to avoid all glazed, shiny, and glossy fabrics, because their sheen is a harsh note in the tapestry of nature's rich and soft coloring. Everything about the outdoor play for children, its theme, its colors, its textures, should have the quality of sympathy with woods and fields. Plain fabrics, such as gingham, and other soft cottons in the desired colors, will blend well with the greenery. The best and most effective figured fabric for outdoor costuming is cretonne, which splashes itself as unexpectedly and vividly with color as does a garden. Cretonnes and chintzes may be used in innumerable ways and a variety of lines, for hangings, trimmings, rugs, and almost any dress of the country or fairy play.

No lighting save incidental effects that glimmer or sparkle should be employed. Lanterns and torches take the roof off the child's outdoor theater; its spacious covering of clouds and sky give to the play a freedom and breadth impossible to obtain indoors. Small lights may be strung among the trees at twilight if necessary, and a spotlight may be thrown upon some important scene for a moment, but daylight and sunshine are our natural lights. Another consideration is that of stage perspective, which artificial lights destroy. The value in education of the outdoor play for children is its spacious, more generous action. The players interpret the characterization at freer distances from one another. The costumes, speech, stage setting and action are all planned for the greater scope of earth, sky and air. This form of dramatization is the oldest, yet always new, since it adapts its lines and pantomime to the limitless stage of the earth.

Shakespeare may be acted outdoors by children of eight to twelve years with success and advantage if adapted by the understanding teacher. "Midsummer Night's Dream" always commends itself to us for child interpretation, but when we study it from the point of human appeal we realize that it is not truly a child's thought. Rather it interprets for the adult the pagan period of the childhood of the race. To my mind "As You Like It" would be interesting for a wider school dramatization than it now enjoys, its love scenes and the long speeches cut. It thrills with the spirit and joy of the forest, just as the child thrills when school is over, and he is free to run away to the woods and take on a new character for himself for closer kinship with nature. "As You Like It" is fuller of understandable situations for a child, innocuous fun, and healthy precepts than many outdoor plays we now use from modern sources. Josephine Preston Peabody's "The Piper" plays itself into the heart of childhood outdoors; it has the quality of the pageant combined with the literary form of the drama. "Old King Cole" makes a joyous garden or field play, its various scenes and situations adapting themselves well to the costuming and action of younger children.

And there is a wealth of play material in folk games and country dances which find a sympathetic place for themselves outdoors where they had their beginnings and to which their steps and rhythms are most happily adapted.

The outdoor theater will also be found inspirational for children's spontaneous dramatizations. They will make their favorite legends of forest and garden into original plays.

PAGEANTRY AND THE COUNTRY SCHOOL

By JOY HIGGINS

Pageantry belongs to the country school. The school in a large city must necessarily interpret drama with limited vision because of the isolation of city life from the contacts of the self-sustaining community. We may argue that no community is any longer self-sustaining; but the country village or town where there is access to local history, where there are old residents who remember the traditions of the place, and where the elemental processes of raising food or manufacturing the necessities of life may be observed, offers invaluable source material for the school play or pantomime. All drama, and notably school drama, should play upon the recognized scale of a people's environment; it should stimulate the imagination through the fairy play, or present an interpretation of life through history. Child drama, as well as adult, should also inspire in both actors and audience a feeling for beauty; color, rhythm, music, stage setting and the movement of the players may all contribute to this inspiration.

The rural school, whether one room or made up of many, has then a great opportunity for the dramatization of a play or better still the pageant. The production may be indoors or outdoors; include a few pupils or the entire school. There is a fine opportunity here for interesting the community in the school as parents and neighbors are invited to see re-enacted through the historical pageant interesting incidents of community history. Town history, from the struggles of the first settlers to the present place of the town in American life, offers the best patriotic theme for the school pageant.

There must be first a definite idea for the play or pageant, detailed and possible of development, with limited resources right at hand. If there are younger pupils only who will take part, any fairy story of universal appeal may be selected, and it will probably need an outdoor setting, which will renew the children's interest in their own neighborhood. The costumes, accessories and dialogue or tableaux may be taken from any of the beautiful books to be found now in every library, authentic in pictorial detail. The pageant from history is better, however, for the country school as it correlates, in research and preparation, with nearly all the school subjects and small children may be used in all the different episodes. We may, therefore, make a plan for such a pageant from local history, which is equally applicable to a story-book pageant, if desired.

Once the theme is chosen, which we may call "The Story of Our Town," all the pupils in the school are considered for their individual ability and divided into committees. Those who show interest in history and geography, together with ability and vision in research, will consult town records, find volumes of early vital statistics, look up the minutes of old town and church meetings, study books of local history in the public library and in private collections, talk with old residents and any neighborhood writer or artist who has made a study of "local color." This committee of pupils will need to develop a large degree of leadership, for upon their information and their insight in selecting the most colorful and significant episodes in the history of the town will depend the beauty of the pageant. Was a hill, a fertile valley or a river course the reason for selecting the site? Were the founders of the community from Europe; were they discoverers, pioneers, or did they come from another near-by settlement because "our town" offered them better chances to work and live happily? If it is a town of foreigners, why and from what country did they come? What made our town grow? All these facts and many more will open the children's eyes to a series of human pictures, a panorama of life, that is the only real background of the pageant.

Next in importance to the committee on history, will be the committee on stage settings, properties and costumes. This group may well be divided, the boys planning to build the stage, make scenery which the committee on art will paint, and collect or make those furnishing accessories needed in the production. The girls will consult with the research group for the costume ideas, procure patterns and cheap materials for these and cut and make them. The art committee will help with dyeing and decorating the costumes with paint and applied designs. Make-up and the details of stage lighting, if the pageant is to be given at night, may also be taken care of by individuals of this group of boys and girls.

Old houses of the town will supply pieces of antique furniture, draperies, patched quilts, period dresses and many other helps. There may also be ancient diaries and letters collected by the town

historical society or in some families that will be
suggestive of episodes, or may be read during the
pageant. The costuming is a simple matter as
period patterns may now be obtained from several
large dress-pattern companies. Mill ends of cotton may be dyed in vivid colors with aniline dyes;
cheesecloth and lawns are easily dipped in solutions
of colored soaps for dyeing dancing costumes. In
large cities there are costumers who will supply
the dress of almost any period, and also booklets
with pictures showing these costumes which may
be used as models. The mothers of the children
will be happy to help if this costume-making is
too much for the school, but if the teacher chooses
her committee well so far as ability in design and
sewing is concerned, and enough time is allowed
for the project, all will go well. Heavy cotton is
an excellent material for almost any use as it dyes
well and may be painted. Medallions or other
decorations of cambric or paper pasted on simulate brocade designs.

The music committee needs to be carefully chosen,
consisting of those pupils who have a feeling for
rhythm and melody, who can organize a chorus
and select folk dances which may be incidental to
the tableaux. If there are children of foreign
parentage in the school, an interesting opportunity
is afforded for introducing their native dances and
folk tunes, in this way interesting their parents
and showing the American-born child the contri-
bution these other children, so often out of place in
the country school, may make to American life.
There may be a town fiddler, harmonica player or a
town band to call upon for incidental music. The
local singing society may be willing to give early

American songs.* Making these contacts, study-
ing the possibilities for music right at hand, and
planning the music program will be among the
richest of the pageant activities.

The group of children who form an art committee
will find their activities varied and closely bound
up with all the others. Choosing the right outdoor spot for the production, painting backgrounds
for either indoor or outdoor sets, and making the
programs will fall to them. The programs may be
printed or hektographed sheets folded once and
bound between decorated covers. The covers may
have applied cut-paper or painted designs suitable
to the time of year, either suggestive of patriotism
or of vacation. Another delightful form of program utilizes snapshots of local interest, the oldest
house in town, the fort, the schoolhouse, the town
hall or soldiers' monument, mounted on the program
cover and inclosed in a decorative border. A
program for the pageant may be outlined as follows:

THE STORY OF OUR TOWN

A Pageant

Given by the Pupils of the —— School

Executive Committee
*
Committee on History
*
Committee on Staging and
Costumes
*
Committee on Art and Programs
*
Music Committee
*
Program

* "American Song Bag," by Carl Sandberg; Harcourt, Brace and Co.

Every community has a historic character, a soldier or an old resident who can tell traditional stories, or an official who has made a study of the history of the town. The services of this person as the Interpreter should be engaged to give the prologue and perhaps a brief description before each episode. The parts of the pageant should be arranged as tableaux, either static or moving as in pantomime. Between the episodes there are recitations appropriate to the theme, dances and musical selections or songs. Descendants of the founders of the community may impersonate their ancestors. Each episode will have a relation to the one that went before and lead up to the following one. The whole production should be exceedingly simple and clear in its meaning, expressing the human interest in history as is possible in no other form of the drama. Monotony is avoided by breaking up the groups of the tableaux, changing the stage picture as the actors enter and exit. There may be a skirmish with Indians, the coming of explorers, always an opening and climax to each episode. Stretch a point so far as color is concerned. If the production is given outdoors, we must contrast or complement the colors of nature to be effective.

The teacher will find the making of a book of the pageant a fruitful activity for the school. In this book each tableau is described and pictured or diagrammed before it is given. The grouping of the players, their movement and gestures, their costumes, the accessories and the stage settings, are written down after having been planned. Each episode is thus assembled and the breaking up of the picture into movement is visualized for the effect upon the audience. If this book of the pageant is so carefully planned by the pupils that it may be kept, it will be a record in correlation of subject-matter with history that should give new impulse to the study.

Pageantry in childhood, under skilled and under-standing leadership, is a means of teaching realism in art. The pageant may develop a sense of beauty in the appreciation of color, pictures, music and rhythmic patterns. The essential symbolic basis, the opportunity offered for experimentation in art, the inspiration through color and music, are educational in the liberal sense of the term. We have not yet realized the possibilities of this form of drama in the country school.

Mother Goose Opens Her Door

By Clara Swain Green

THE PLAYERS

MOTHER GOOSE.
BO-PEEP.
JACK AND JILL.
MISS MUFFET.
JACK HORNER.
MARY, QUITE CONTRARY, AND HER NEIGHBOR.
JACK SPRAT AND WIFE.
QUEEN AND JACK OF HEARTS.
MOTHER HUBBARD.
DR. FOSTER.
NANCY ETTICOAT.
TOMMY TUCKER.

MOTHER GOOSE OPENS HER DOOR

By Clara Swain Green

THE COSTUMING

Use as many and gay colors as possible. The materials used may be crepe paper, soft cambric and figured cottons.

The character of Mother Goose is taken by an older person, mother or teacher, whose presence will give the little ones confidence. She wears a black pointed hat and long black cape. The other players are costumed as follows:

Bo-Peep. White dress over which is worn a little black laced bodice. Cretonne is draped for the skirt to give pannier effect. She carries a crook.

Boy Blue. A bright blue costume consisting of a smock and long full trousers. He wears a straw hat and carries a horn.

Jack and Jill. Jack wears short green trousers, a jacket, "Eton" style, of black and a cap of green. Jill is dressed in a full short green skirt, a black jacket, and a green hat. They carry a very large pail.

Miss Muffet. A flowered gown of ankle length trimmed with bright yellow ruffles, and a yellow sun-bonnet. She carries a bowl containing dry cereal and a spoon.

Jack Horner. Wears a bright purple "Oliver Twist" suit with huge white collar, cuffs, and belt. He carries a Christmas pie.

Mary, Quite Contrary, is dressed in old-fashioned costume of pink hoop-skirt effect. She wears white pantalettes, black mitts and a flower-trimmed hat, and carries a flower pot. Her Neighbor has a suit of black sateen with long tailed coat and long trousers. White ruffles trim the front of the coat and edge the wrists. He wears a man's black silk hat and carries a cane.

Jack Sprat, who is a tiny boy, may wear the present-day suit of long trousers, coat and vest so popular for small boys, a derby hat and carry a cane. Jack's Wife, a very small, plump girl, wears a long gown of pale blue, a white apron, kerchief and cap.

QUEEN OF HEARTS. A long white dress covered with red paper hearts. A long train is fastened from her shoulders. She wears a gilt crown and carries a rolling pin.

JACK OF HEARTS. A boy's suit of white linen to which red hearts are sewed. A short red cape hangs from his shoulders. He wears a red "tam" with a white plume.

OLD MOTHER HUBBARD. Black cape and hood trimmed with orange ruffles. Cotton batting stitched inside of hood represents her white hair. A pet dog on a leash accompanies her.

DR. FOSTER. Long trousers and long tailed coat, silk hat, spectacles. He carries an umbrella and a medicine case.

NANCY ETTICOAT. Flounced red crepe paper dress. Wears a flat hat made of ruffles stitched or pasted on cardboard. From the middle of the hat, a large white paper candle with an orange wick rises.

TOMMY TUCKER. "Oliver Twist" suit of buff cotton with a large white bib. He carries an empty dish and spoon.

STAGE DIRECTIONS

At one side are placed: a small table, an artificial spider, a platter, tart tins, a hassock, a cupboard.

The artificial spider should be very large. One may be made of a black silk stocking cut in the shape of a spider's body, the stuffed legs wired and bright colored beads used as eyes. A string is attached to the spider and it is slowly pulled toward Miss Muffet by a person concealed on the other side of the stage.

The music is continuous, changing as the different characters appear. A piano placed at one side will not interfere and the musician can watch the opening and closing of Mother Goose's door.

When the curtain rises this door, covered with black or cream colored cambric, is seen at the back of the stage. On it is pasted in large white letters, the title, "The Book of Mother Goose." A white silhouette of a goose placed below the lettering will add to the effect. A brass knocker borrowed for the occasion will be attractive. Green trees in tubs may stand at either side of the door. The stage itself is covered with green.

During Mother Goose's entrance "Rock-A-Bye-Baby" is played, continuing while she recites. As the lullaby is played

the door opens gently and Mother Goose peers through.   Each
character holds the pose for a moment in the doorway as he **or**
she appears.   Mother Goose advances to the front of the stage.

THE ACTION OF THE PANTOMIME

MOTHER GOOSE (*reciting in time to music*):

Long years ago when I was young,
    And sat on mother's knee,
The tales she told from Mother Goose
    Were very real to me.
In fancy I saw every one
    Peep from out the book,
And now today we'll glance again
    To see just how they look.

(MOTHER GOOSE *returns to the door.   Just before she opens
it she announces* BO-PEEP. BO-PEEP *poses for a moment in the
doorway.*)

MOTHER GOOSE:

Little Bo-Peep has lost her sheep,
    And doesn't know where to find them.
Leave them alone and they'll come home,
    Dragging their tails behind them.

(*As* BO-PEEP *steps out* MOTHER GOOSE *closes the door.*
BO-PEEP *advances to the front of the stage, shading her eyes with
her hand, looking for her sheep.   She may also put her hand to
her mouth as though calling.   As her imaginary flock returns,
she welcomes each sheep and lamb and goes through the pantomime
of folding them.   Exit* BO-PEEP.)

MOTHER GOOSE (*announces* BOY BLUE, *opens the door
and discloses* BOY BLUE *posed there*):

Little Boy Blue, come blow your horn,
    Sheep are in the meadow,
The cows are in the corn.
    Oh, where is the little boy
Who watches the sheep?
    Under the haystack, fast asleep.

(LITTLE BOY BLUE *comes out seeming very sleepy, rubbing his eyes and yawning. Finally he sits down, then lies down and goes to sleep. He hears someone calling off-stage and jumps up in alarm. Makes motion of blowing on his horn. Exit* BOY BLUE.)

MOTHER GOOSE (*stands back-stage through this pantomime. Announces* JACK *and* JILL. *She opens door.*):

Jack and Jill went up the hill,
    To get a pail of water,
Jack fell down and broke his crown
    And Jill came tumbling after.

(JACK *and* JILL *take high steps as though climbing a hill. Suddenly* JACK *stumbles and falls.* JILL *tumbles too on top of* JACK. JACK *jumps up and ruefully rubs his head,* JILL *her nose. Exit* JACK *and* JILL.)

MOTHER GOOSE (*places a small hassock in center, front of stage. Announces* MISS MUFFET.):

Little Miss Muffet sat on a tuffet
    Eating her curds and whey,
When along came a spider
And sat down beside her,
    Which frightened Miss Muffet away.

(MISS MUFFET *seats herself on the hassock and is busily engaged in eating when the "spider," operated from off-stage, reaches her side. She jumps up in great fright. Starts to cry, drops her bowl and spoon and runs off the stage.*)

MOTHER GOOSE (*clears stage for the next pantomime, goes to the door and announces* LITTLE JACK HORNER *and opens the door*):

Little Jack Horner, sat in a corner,
    Eating his Christmas pie.
He stuck in his thumb,
Pulled out a plum,
    And said, "What a big boy am I!"

(JACK *goes to the corner and seats himself on the hassock. He holds the pie in his lap. The pie may be a basin covered over the top with brown paper. A red ribbon is tied around it. He sticks his thumb through the paper and pulls out a plum, a fig or date, which he immediately eats. Exit* JACK HORNER.)

MOTHER GOOSE (*announces* MARY, MARY, QUITE
CONTRARY *and her* NEIGHBOR. *She opens the door.*):
> Mistress Mary, Quite Contrary,
>> How does your garden grow?
> With silver bells and cockle shells,
>> And pretty maids all in a row.

(*The* LITTLE BOY NEIGHBOR *steps out of the doorway and with a
very courtly bow doffs his hat.* MARY *curtsies in reply. He
takes her hand, holding it high, and leads her out. She at once
brushes him aside and trips over to an imaginary garden at the
side of the stage where she pretends to fill the flower pot which she
carries with earth. The little boy now approaches her and bows.
She curtsies and they take the steps of an old-fashioned minuet.
Exit* MARY *and her* NEIGHBOR.)

MOTHER GOOSE (*places a small table and two chairs in
center of stage. On the table rests a large platter of candy in the
shape of meat. She announces* JACK SPRAT *and his* WIFE.
Opens the door.):
> Jack Sprat could eat no fat,
>> His wife could eat no lean,
> And so between them both, you see,
>> They left the platter clean.

(JACK'S WIFE *holds his arm.* JACK *pulls out her chair and
seats her, then himself. They proceed to eat from the platter.
Finally leave it empty. Exit* JACK SPRAT *and his* WIFE.)

MOTHER GOOSE (*removes the chairs and platter, substitut-
ing on the table two tart tins and some plasteline dough, and says,
The* QUEEN *and the* JACK OF HEARTS):
> The Queen of Hearts made some tarts
>> Upon a summer day.
> The Jack of Hearts stole those tarts
>> And with them ran away.

(*The* QUEEN *steps out alone, goes to the table and using her
rolling pin and the dough makes some tarts. Then appearing
warm and tired, steps over to the side with her back to the table and
slowly fans herself.* JACK OF HEARTS *softly steals up and snatches
the tarts just as he passes the* QUEEN. *She sees him and chases
him. Exit the* QUEEN *and* JACK OF HEARTS.)

MOTHER GOOSE (*removes the table and announces* OLD MOTHER HUBBARD):

Old Mother Hubbard went to the cupboard
  To get her poor dog a bone,
When she got there the cupboard was bare,
  And so the poor dog had none.

(OLD MOTHER HUBBARD *enters and leads her dog around the stage. A toy dog on wheels may be used. At last she goes to a small cupboard at back and right of stage, pulls out several dishes and shakes her head mournfully when she discovers they are empty. Throws up her hands in a gesture of despair. Exit* OLD MOTHER HUBBARD.)

MOTHER GOOSE (*announces* DR. FOSTER *and opens door*):

Dr. Foster went to Gloucester
  In a pouring rain,
Stepped in a puddle
Up to his middle,
  And will not go there again.

(DR. FOSTER *steps out, sets down his medicine case and opens his umbrella, picks up his case and walks towards stage center. Suddenly his feet fly out from under him and he sits down. He rises and brushes off his clothes. Exit* DR. FOSTER.)

MOTHER GOOSE (*announces* LITTLE NANCY ETTICOAT):

Little Nancy Etticoat in a red petticoat
  And a long nose;
The longer she stands
The shorter she grows.

(LITTLE NANCY ETTICOAT *dances out to center stage on her toes with her arms extended stiffly sideways. She very slowly drops her arms, at the same time lowering her body, until she is in a kneeling position with her head drooping. Exit* NANCY ETTICOAT.)

MOTHER GOOSE (*announces* TOMMY TUCKER. *While* TOMMY *holds pose she recites*):

Little Tommy Tucker sang for his supper.
What shall he have? White bread and butter.
How shall he cut it without any knife?
How will he marry without any wife?

(TOMMY *advances to the front of the stage pretending to cry and holding out his empty dish. Then he stops and smiles and begins to sing in pantomime. Exit* TOMMY TUCKER *followed by* MOTHER GOOSE.)

(*As the music changes to a march the players re-enter through the door in couples led by* MOTHER GOOSE *as follows*)

> Nancy Etticoat and Tommy Tucker
> Mother Hubbard and Dr. Foster
> Queen of Hearts and Jack of Hearts
> Jack Sprat's Wife and Jack Sprat
> Mistress Mary and Her Neighbor
> Miss Muffet and Jack Horner
> Jill and Jack
> Bo-Peep and Boy Blue

(*A very short marching drill or folk dance may be given. This shows the contrasting costumes and can be easily arranged with the leadership of* MOTHER GOOSE.)

MUSIC FOR THE PANTOMIME

Little Bo-Peep.....................*Any old-fashioned polka*
Little Boy Blue........................."*The Shepherd Boy*"
Little Miss Muffet........................."*Humoresque*"
Old Mother Hubbard..."*Oh, Where Has My Little Dog Gone?*"
Jack and Jill............................"*Yankee Doodle*"
Mistress Mary...."*You're Just a Flower from An Old Bouquet*"
Jack Sprat and Wife.....................*Stephanie Gavotte*
Little Jack Horner........................."*Jingle Bells*"
Dr. Foster................."*It Ain't Gonna Rain No Mo'!*"
Nancy Etticoat.................."*Kisses of Spring*," *Waltz*
Little Tommy Tucker.............."*Love's Old Sweet Song*"
Queen and Jack of Hearts............."*Hearts and Flowers*"
Incidental Music............."*Mother Goose Suite*," *Ravel*
Four Mother Goose Rhythms.................*Arthur Nevin*
Mother Goose's Nursery Rhymes Set to Music....*J. W. Elliott*

Five-Minute Plays
By Rebecca Rice

FIVE–MINUTE PLAYS

By Rebecca Rice

These dramatizations from Æsop's Fables have proved most attractive to younger children, who seem to feel that it is a real treat to play them. They can be acted with no special costuming or scenery, or may be produced more elaborately if desired.

Costumes do, of course, add much to the children's enjoyment, and, if the plays are to be put on before an audience, are usually necessary. The best plan is to correlate these dramatizations with drawing and let the children make masks. If the teacher or parent desires to present these plays formally and does not mind a little bother and expense, gray flannel or cambric suits might be made for the mice, a green one for the grasshopper, black ones for the ants, and reddish-brown ones for foxes. The foxes' tails may be made from crepe paper.

As the Æsop Fables are Greek, and as Greek drama was distinguished by little or no scenery, an outdoor setting in the playground or garden is suitable.

THE GRASSHOPPER AND THE ANT

Act I.
    Time—Summer.
    Place—Meadow.
    Players—Grasshopper, Ant.

Act II.
    Time—Winter.
    Place—Ant's Home.
    Players—Grasshopper, Mr. Ant, Mrs. Ant, Tiny, Busy.

ACT I

(Mrs. Ant *is busily picking up food.* Mr. Grasshopper *dances in, playing a fiddle and humming. He goes over to* Mrs. Ant.)

Mr. Grasshopper: Good morning, Mrs. Ant. What are you doing?

Mrs. Ant: I am picking up food to store away for the winter.

Mr. Grasshopper: Won't you come and play with me? I will play my fiddle and we will dance. This is too nice a day to work.

Mrs. Ant (*shaking head*): Indeed, I can't come and dance with you. I must work, for winter is coming and I must have food for my family.

Mr. Grasshopper: Why worry about winter? Winter is a long way off. Surely you do not need to work today. Let winter take care of itself.

Mrs. Ant: Winter is not a long time off. It will soon be here and if I do not get this grain in I will be hungry later. I advise you to go to work too, for if you do not work now you will worry later.

Mr. Grasshopper: Pooh, I am not going to work

on such a beautiful day as this. I will skip, and dance, and play through this happy summer day. You see I am a poet as well as a musician and a dancer. Good-by, Mrs. Ant. I think that you are a very dull person.

MRS. ANT: Good-by, you silly fellow. Mark my words, you will be sorry later.

MR. GRASSHOPPER (*dancing off*):

> I am happy, I am gay,
> I dance trouble
> And care away.

What a stupid person Mrs. Ant is. What do I care for winter!

ACT II

(MRS. ANT *is setting her supper table.* MR. ANT *is watching her. The children are playing on the floor.*)

MR. ANT: Isn't supper almost ready? I'm starved!

MRS. ANT: It will be ready very soon, my dear, for I am setting the table. Come, children, stop your play and get ready for supper. Brush your gay coats till they shine and don't forget your wings.

TINY: Yes, Mother.

BUSY: I am hungry. (*They draw up to the table.*) How good everything looks.

MR. ANT: Let me help you to a nice bit of corn. It is perfectly delicious.
(*A knock is heard at the door.*)

MRS. ANT: Run to the door, Tiny. See who it is.

TINY (*goes to door and lets* MR. GRASSHOPPER *in*): It is Mr. Grasshopper, Mother.

Mrs. Ant: How do you do, Mr. Grasshopper? You do not look as well as you did this summer. What do you want?

Mr. Grasshopper: Oh, Mrs. Ant, take pity on a starving fellow and give me some of your food. I have not eaten for two days. Please give me just a little corn.

Mrs. Ant: Corn? I have no extra corn. When it was summer I worked hard in the fields to get enough for the winter. Day after day I toiled in the hot sun. What were you doing when food was plentiful?

Mr. Grasshopper: I played in the fields. I danced and sang all day.

Mrs. Ant: Alas, you foolish fellow, I have no food for you. You said that you danced and sang all summer? Now go and dance the winter away.

(Mr. Grasshopper, *looking wiser, exits.*)

THE FOX AND HIS TAIL

Players—Fox, called Bushy Tail; His Four Brothers.

Fox (*looking regretfully at the place where his tail should be*): Alas, I have lost my tail in a sharp trap. How strange I look without it, and how my brothers will tease and laugh at me! If only I could make them want to have their tails cut off too. (*Looks up.*) Here they come now. I will place myself against this tree so they will not see my loss.

First Brother: How do you do, Bushy Tail?

Fox: Nicely, thank you. How hot you look!

First Brother: It is a warm day.

Fox: Yes, it is hot. I have often thought that it is our tails that make us so warm. Think how long and bushy they are.

First Brother: I suppose you are right. Our tails are very warm.

Fox (*turning toward* Second Brother): You look very tired.

Second Brother: Why, maybe I am, for I have been running all morning.

Fox: How heavy our tails are. I sometimes get very tired carrying mine about. Really, when the dogs are after us we could run much faster without tails.

Second Brother: You are right. I often get tired of carrying my tail upright. Then I have to let it trail.

Fox: What is that which you have in your tail, Reddy?

Third Brother: It is a burdock. It is all tangled up in the hairs and I cannot get it out. I have been biting at it all morning, but all I can succeed in doing is pulling my own hair.

Fox: It is so hard to keep tails free from burdocks and looking well. A matted tail is no ornament. Don't you think tails are a nuisance? They are hot; they are heavy, they get matted with burdocks, and they catch in things.

Brothers: So they do. Yes.

First Brother: I never realized what a trouble they were till you spoke of it. Why do we carry around such burdens?

Fox: What an excellent suggestion. Bushy Tail suggests we all cut our tails off. I for one think it is a fine idea.

Fourth Brother (*runs around tree looking at* Bushy Tail *keenly*): Oh, ho, brother, I see why you are so eager to have us cut off our beautiful tails. (*He pushes* Bushy Tail *from tree.*) Look, brothers, he has lost his own tail and wants all of us to lose ours in order that he may not be alone in his misfortune.

Others: He has lost his own tail! No wonder he wants us to get rid of ours.

First Brother: No wonder he said tails were warm!

Second Brother: No wonder he said they were heavy!

Third Brother: No wonder he said they were no ornaments!

All: We will keep our tails. We will keep our tails. (Bushy Tail *slinks off, followed by others repeating*) We will keep our tails. We will keep our tails.

BELLING THE CAT

Act I.
    Time—Evening.
    Place—The Pantry Shelf.
    Players—Tidbit, Little Gray, Scamper, Grandpa Big Ears.
(*The mice are seated in a semicircle about some cheese.*)

Tidbit: One day when my Uncle Whiskers was getting me some cheese and cake, the big gray cat came along. He snapped my poor uncle up and he was gone. Oh, how sorry I felt. I shall never see him again.

SCAMPER: Did I tell you what happened to me? I was playing in the leaves. Gray Pussy was hiding under the steps. Just as I was hurrying to my hole that horrid cat bit off the end of my tail. Oh, dear! Just look at it.

TIDBIT: What a shame! It quite spoils your beauty.

SCAMPER: It hurts, too.

LITTLE GRAY: One day I was playing in the cellar. There was something there. I was very frightened. I ran into my hole. My mother said, "What is the matter?" I said, "There is something in the cellar that has shining green eyes." Just then a long paw with claws on it was pushed into our hole and I couldn't say another word. It was the cat. We both had to scamper farther into our hole.

GRANDPA BIG EARS: When I was walking along the pantry shelf, a cat was hiding in the house. Just as I was nibbling at some cheese, he pounced on me. I was terribly frightened. I slipped between his paws and ran away as fast as I could go. You can see the scar which his claws made to this very day.

TIDBIT: It is dreadful! What can we do?

LITTLE GRAY: I know! We will get a bell and tie it about the cat's neck. When the bell rings we will know that the cat is coming.

SCAMPER: That is a splendid plan. I did not know that you were so clever.

TIDBIT: Yes, let us do it.

GRANDPA BIG EARS: Yes, but who is going to tie the bell on the cat's neck?

TIDBIT: Not I!

SCAMPER: Not I!

LITTLE GRAY: Not I!

GRAY PUSSY (*entering softly*): Well, here is my supper.

MICE (*running away*): *Eee-eee-eeek!*

The Land of Play
By Mary Sharpe

THE PLAYERS

LITTLE BOY.
LITTLE RED RIDING HOOD.
THE WOLF.
THE OLD WOMAN.
PIG WHO WOULD NOT JUMP OVER THE STILE.
THE LITTLE RED HEN.
THE GINGERBREAD BOY.
CHICKEN LITTLE.
GREAT BIG BILLY-GOAT-GRUFF.
BIG BILLY-GOAT-GRUFF.
LITTLE BILLY-GOAT-GRUFF.
GOLDILOCKS.
LITTLE BLACK SAMBO.
PETER RABBIT.

PLACE—The Forest of Story Books.

THE LAND OF PLAY

By MARY SHARPE

STAGE DIRECTIONS

The forest is represented by a floor covering of green denim or heavy cambric on which artificial flowers made by the children are scattered. A back drop of green or brown cloth upon which the trunks of trees are painted would add to the realism of the forest. If it is not possible to make this, two screens covered with a forest color will provide a background and stage entrance. There is a wide opening in the center, with a path leading from the back of the stage to a small green-covered hummock beside which Little Boy sits. He holds an open picture book and there are other story books piled near. If the play is given outdoors the setting may be beautiful. It should be played on the edge of a woodland with only a row of stones to separate the children who watch from the Players.

COSTUMING

Little Boy wears his everyday clothes. The other players dress as nearly as possible like their pictures in Little Boy's story books. Those who are animals wear masks. Ordinary toy masks may be used. If any character change is needed, make it with clay on the surface of the mask and paint with showcard colors. The rabbit mask should have long flannel ears lined and stiffened with pink cambric. The Billy-Goats-Gruff wear masks to which are attached rolled paper horns of long, middle size, and short lengths. Great Big Billy-Goat-Gruff may wish a beard, which can be made of fringed paper or rope and glued to his mask. Goldilocks has long yellow hair. Chicken Little, who is a small child, has wings of yellow paper feathers fastened to the shoulders of his blouse, and his mask has a yellow beak. Little Red Hen has red wings and topknot. The Gingerbread Boy wears an all-over suit of brown cambric.

ACCESSORIES

Little Red Riding Hood's basket filled with small cakes. The Old Woman's staff, which is a huge candy stick. Little Red

Hen's loaf of bread. A real gingerbread boy. Goldilock's porridge bowl and spoon. Chicken Little's pieces of the sky, which are bits of blue or pink paper he carries in his pocket or conceals in one hand. Little Black Sambo's umbrella and a toy tiger. Peter Rabbit's dinner from Mr. McGregor's garden, a bunch of carrots and other vegetables.

SCENE I

(LITTLE BOY *is seen looking at his story books. As he turns the pages, softly played music from MacDowell's "Woodland Sketches" is heard.*)

LITTLE BOY:

"When at books alone I sit
And I am very tired of it,
I have just to shut my eyes
To go sailing through the skies,
To go sailing far away
To the pleasant Land of Play;
To the fairyland afar
Where the Little People are."

That would be fun, but of course it couldn't happen. There isn't any Land of Play with Little People in it.

(*There is again the sound of soft music, this time a lullaby.*)

LITTLE BOY: How I should love to see the Story People. (*Yawns.*) It is warm and drowsy here in the woods. I could shut my eyes and take a nap until it is time to go home.

(*He closes his eyes, leans back, and is soon fast asleep. LITTLE RED RIDING HOOD is seen peeping in through the entrance at the back. She steps through, looking about to see that no one is watching her, and comes along the path.*)

LITTLE RED RIDING HOOD: Oh, I'm so warm, but I shouldn't stop here. Mother said to go straight to Grandmother's house. But these flowers are so pretty. I know Grandmother would like them as well as the cake I have in my basket. (*She stops to gather some flowers; raises her head; sees a wolf approaching.*) Oh, dear, there is Mr. Wolf! I wonder what he wants.

WOLF (*speaking in a gruff voice*): Hello, Little Red Riding Hood. What are you doing here?

RED RIDING HOOD: I am on my way to Grandmother's house with a basket of cakes. Don't eat me up! (*She turns as if to run away.*)

WOLF: Don't you know, Red Riding Hood, that I could not hurt you here even if I wanted to? This is

"The fairyland afar
Where the Little People are."

If you stay here with me you will see many strange sights.

RED RIDING HOOD: Truly? My Grandmother may not be at home. I have always wished I might see Fairyland. (*She comes closer to* WOLF *and pats him.*

WOLF: We can eat a cake so as not to waste them. (*They sit down by a tree in the forest and start eating. The* OLD WOMAN *and her* PIG *enter. The* PIG *comes in first, very slowly and heavily.* OLD WOMAN *beats him with her staff.*)

OLD WOMAN: Stick, stick, beat Pig! I see by the moonlight it's long past midnight. Time Pig and I were home an hour and a half ago.

(PIG *sits down at side of stage and begins to grunt.* OLD WOMAN *wrings her hands in despair. Wipes her face with her apron. Suddenly sees* LITTLE RED RIDING HOOD.)

OLD WOMAN: Can you tell me how I can make Pig jump over the stile, so I can get home tonight?

I have asked the stick, fire, and water, but they cannot help me.

WOLF: Stop a while with us. What is the need of going home? Why not stay here in the Land of Play? Red Riding Hood will give Pig a part of her cake. Maybe then he will not be so stubborn. Perhaps you can get him home in the morning.

OLD WOMAN: We may as well stay here, I suppose; that is, if I can have my supper. (*She joins* RED RIDING HOOD, *who shares a cake with* OLD WOMAN *and* PIG.) Listen, what a noise! I wonder who it can be! Such a funny looking couple is coming! (*They run and look down the path.*)

WOLF: Oh, I know the one in front. That is the Gingerbread Boy, but I thought my cousin, the fox, ate him. (*The* GINGERBREAD BOY *and* CHICKEN LITTLE *enter with a noise back-stage of clattering tinware and the cluckings of fowls.*)

ALL: Why are you running away?

GINGERBREAD BOY: I ran away from a little old woman, a little old man. I ran away from a pig. And I can—

PIG (*rousing*): You may have run away once but you can't now.

GINGERBREAD BOY: Then I may as well rest a while before I start on again. What about Chicken Little whom I have here? He is trying to find some one to help him keep the sky from falling.

PIG: How does he know the sky is falling?

CHICKEN LITTLE: I saw it with my eyes. I heard it with my ears. Some of it fell on my tail.

OLD WOMAN: You are just about as queer as

Pig. He won't jump over the stile. I can't get home tonight. You and Gingerbread Boy had better stay here for supper. You can both start home with Pig and me in the morning.

CHICKEN LITTLE (*eering abou in the forest*): The sky won't fall here. The trees would catch it.

GINGERBREAD BOY: I don't suppose either Pig or Wolf will eat me in this Land of Play.

(*The Players gather in a friendly way about* LITTLE RED RIDING HOOD *and she feeds them from her basket. They do not see* LITTLE BOY.)

SCENE II

(*The supper the Story Book Players are enjoying is interrupted by a heavy tramping of feet and a loud rumbling noise off-stage. They look up startled.* LITTLE RED RIDING HOOD *runs to the entrance at the back of the stage and looks up the road.*)

RED RIDING HOOD: Such a noise! It sounds like thunder. (*The* BILLY-GOATS-GRUFF *come in sight.*)

ALL (*joining* RED RID IG HOOD): Why, there are the three Billy-Goats-Gruff. (GREAT BIG BILLY-GOAT-GRUFF, BIG BILLY-GOAT-GRUFF, *and* LITTLE BILLY-GOAT-GRUFF *enter the forest.*)

GREAT BIG BILLY-GOAT-GRUFF (*speaking in a deep voice*): Are there any more trolls here? I knocked one off the bridge with my big horns. (*He sees the* WOLF.) I can chase you out of this forest, too. *Runs toward* WOLF.)

WOLF: Stop! This is the Land of Play. No one fights here. Where have you and your brothers been?

LITTLE BILLY-GOAT-GRUFF (*speaking in a wee voice*): We are on our way home. We have been over to the hillside. There we ate all the grass we could hold. See how fat we are! (*All three swell up with pride.*)

WOLF: Then stay with us. You will see stranger sights here than trolls.

BIG BILLY-GOAT-GRUFF: After good eating comes good resting.

LITTLE BILLY-GOAT-GRUFF: Guess whom we met on our way?

OLD WOMAN: Was it some one who could persuade this Pig of mine to jump over the stile?

LITTLE BILLY-GOAT-GRUFF: No, it was Little Red Hen. She couldn't help you, for she was trying to plant a grain of wheat. Why, here she is now. (LITTLE RED HEN *seems to be hunting for something as she enters.*)

OLD WOMAN: Can I help you?

LITTLE RED HEN (*starting in surprise*): Oh, if you will be so kind, perhaps you will find a place for me to plant this grain of wheat. If I plant it, cut it, thresh it, and grind it into flour, I shall have a loaf of bread.

RED RIDING HOOD: Here is a place to plant your wheat. (*She shows* RED HEN *a spot back of Little Boy's hummock, but neither see him.* LITTLE RED HEN *plants wheat.*)

OLD WOMAN: Red Riding Hood, it must be time for some one else to come. In a forest like this, something is always happening.

WOLF: Woof! Woof! Why not listen to me bark. I can be very fierce indeed if I like. (*He prances about barking.*)

(GOLDILOCKS *peers through the entrance to the stage, sees* WOLF, *and runs away. She returns soon accompanied by* LITTLE BLACK SAMBO. *He wears purple bed slippers, carries a green umbrella, and has a toy tiger which he drags along behind him. He holds*

GOLDILOCKS' *arm protectingly and covers her with his umbrella as they enter.*)

OLD WOMAN: Here come Goldilocks and Little Black Sambo! I met Goldilocks this morning. She told me about running away from the Three Bears.

GREAT BIG BILLY-GOAT-GRUFF (*speaking in a gruff voice*): Who is Goldilocks? She must be a "fraid cat." Bears are nothing compared with a troll with eyes as big as this. (*Makes a ring with his fingers around his eyes as large as possible.*)

LITTLE BILLY-GOAT-GRUFF (*softly*): Are you that little girl who ran away from bears?

GOLDILOCKS: Yes, I am. Such bears! Such voices! (*Pretends to dip from her porridge bowl and imitates the voices of the big, the middle-size, and the tiny bear.*)

SOMEBODY HAS BEEN EATING MY PORRIDGE.

SOMEBODY HAS BEEN EATING MY PORRIDGE.

SOMEBODY HAS BEEN EATING MY PORRIDGE.

LITTLE BLACK SAMBO: Bears are nothing to tigers. Four striped tigers came rolling and tumbling right to the very tree where I was hiding from them in the jungle, but I jumped quickly behind my umbrella. Then the tigers all caught hold of each other's tails saying *gr-r-r-rrr*. And so they found themselves in a ring around the tree. And they ran around the tree trying to eat each other up, and they ran faster and faster until they were whirling so fast that you couldn't see their legs at all.

And still they ran faster and faster until they all just melted away and nothing was left but a great big pool of melted butter at the foot of the tree. And my mother saw all that melted butter and she said, "Now we shall have pancakes for supper."

CHICKEN LITTLE: Well, I am the one who thought that the sky was falling. One day when I was out in the rose garden something fell on my tail. So I ran away to tell Henny Penny and Ducky Lucky and Goosey Loosey and Turkey Lurkey that the sky was falling. I saw it with my eyes and heard it with my ears, and a piece of the sky fell on my tail.

OLD WOMAN: Who is that coming down the road in such a hurry?

PIG: That is Peter Rabbit. He is a good friend of mine. I met him once in the garden.

ALL (*speaking to* PETER RABBIT *as he enters*): Why are you in such a hurry?

PETER RABBIT: Mr. McGregor is after me. My father had an accident in his garden. Mrs. McGregor put him into a pie. I just squeezed under his gate. I must get home as fast as I can.

ALL: Nothing will hurt you in this Land of Play.

PETER RABBIT: Perhaps not, but as it is my mother will give me herb tea when I get home. If I am much later, I may get a spanking.

PIG: It is so late that we all had better start home.

OLD WOMAN: If Pig is ready to go, I know that every one else is.

(*The Story Book Players group themselves preparatory to leaving. On their way toward the back of the stage they suddenly discover* LITTLE BOY *who is still asleep. They tiptoe about looking at the picture books, turning the pages and, surprised, find their own pictures. They cautiously form a ring and dance about* LITTLE BOY. *Then they lay offerings at his feet:* RED RIDING HOOD'S *bouquet of wild flowers,* OLD WOMAN'S *candy stick,* LITTLE RED HEN'S *loaf,* GOLDILOCKS' *porridge bowl,* LITTLE BLACK SAMBO'S *toy tiger,* PETER RABBIT'S *bunch of vegetables. They all run off-stage except* CHICKEN LITTLE, *who scatters his pieces of the sky over* LITTLE BOY. *He just escapes, following the others, before* LITTLE BOY *awakes.*)

LITTLE BOY (*wakes up, rubs his eyes, picks up a book and continues his reading*):

"I have played at books that I have read
    Till it is time to go to bed."

(*Discovers the gifts left by the vanished Players. Picks them up. Goes to the stage entrance and looks up and down the road puzzled.*)

LITTLE BOY: It must have been a dream. (*Starts to go home.*) I go to bed with backward looks at my dear land of story books. (*Is about to leave the forest when* LITTLE RED RIDING HOOD *is seen peeping through the trees to see if* LITTLE BOY *liked her flowers. They greet each other happily and spy the other players. All return and join* LITTLE BOY *in a final tableau or simple folk dance.*)

Why Jack-o'-Lantern Keeps Hallowe'en

By Carolyn Sherwin Bailey

THE PLAYERS

October.

A Boy.

Goblins.

Black Cats.

A Girl.

Jack-o'-Lantern.

A Witch.

A Scarecrow.

WHY JACK–O'–LANTERN KEEPS HALLOWE'EN

By Carolyn Sherwin Bailey

THE COSTUMES

October wears a short, straight tunic of fringed brown cotton to the shoulders of which are attached streamers of bright red, yellow, and orange cambric that flutter as she moves. On her head is a chaplet of colored autumn leaves, and she may carry a horn of plenty. She has sandals but no stockings.

The Boy may wear his everyday outdoor clothes. The Girl, also, is dressed as usual. Jack-o'-Lantern has green trailing vines and leaves sewed to an orange cambric suit cut like a child's sleeping garment. Drooping leaves make his headdress and he carries a lighted pumpkin lantern in the second scene.

The Goblins are dressed alike in short, tight breeches and jackets, pointed caps with tassels, and sharp-toed shoes of felt or leather-finished cloth, matching their suits in color. The colors of the costumes differ to give the effect of the forest in October,— scarlet, green, brown, orange, and yellow. Each goblin carries a cloth sack over his back.

Black Cat costumes are easily made of cambric cut like Jack-o'-Lantern's, with the feet and hands covered. Black paper masks with short pointed ears are worn, and attached to the costumes are stuffed tails which the players can move amusingly. These are very small children.

The Scarecrow has as ragged a suit as possible,—old shoes, a battered hat, and straw sticking to his clothes. Any grotesque mask will be suitable. The Witch has the usual tall, peaked hat, a short, full red skirt, a yellow bodice, and a broomstick which she carries under her arm. Upon her shoulder a toy cat perches. The musicians wear farmer's dress,—overalls, checked shirts and straw hats for the boys, gingham dresses and sunbonnets for the girls.

STAGE DIRECTIONS

A farm gate and fence at the back of the stage, which can be made of lathe or strips of heavy strawboard, gives opportunity for entrance and exit. It is wound with lengths of bitter-

sweet and wild cucumber vine.   Wild flowers are banked behind
it.   Strips of theatrical gauze or thin gray cambric to which
waxed autumn leaves are attached hang from the ceiling above
the stage and give an effect of outdoors.   There are heaps of
apples, bright vegetables, ears of yellow corn, and tall corn
shocks about, and the footlights are placed in candlesticks cut
from apples, carrots, and turnips.   Colored leaves, either waxed
or cut from paper, lie on the floor of the stage and blow about as
the players move.   Plainly visible in Scene I are two huge
pumpkins.

The musicians have typical Hallowe'en instruments which
they have made for accompanying the incidental music played
on a piano or victrola.   Most effective of these are the corncob
fiddles.   These are made by selecting a cornstalk that has two
tough joints.   With a sharp knife narrow shreds are cut through
the surface of the stalk on one side, lengthwise from joint to
joint, and lifted from the pith.   This makes the fiddle strings,
under which a low bridge whittled from wood is placed and
moved nearer to the end of the fiddle.   The bow is made of a
smaller stalk in the same way except that the strings are finer
and a low bridge is placed beneath them at both ends.

Cornstalk whistles are included in the orchestra.   An Indian
drum, and a rattle made of a dried gourd filled with large seeds or
small pebbles, are used.   The sound of rushing wind is made by
rubbing the hands across the head of the drum.

The stage lighting, if the play is given in a darkened room,
will have much to do with its realism.   Sunlight is produced
with yellow bulbs for Scene I.   Scene II, which represents
Hallowe'en, should have a white light for moonlight shining
through the leaves and down upon the fruits and vegetables.

The Prologue is given in front of a drop curtain of closely
gathered gauze or cheesecloth in orange, deep purple, or crimson,
the autumn colors.   At either side of the curtain, hiding the
entrance and exit space for the players, are tall jars of golden
rod or asters.

PROLOGUE

*The players, one at a time, appear in front of the drop curtain
and speak, then exit at opposite side.*

OCTOBER:
"Season of mists and mellow fruitfulness!

Close bosom friend of the maturing sun;
Conspiring with him how to load and bless
With fruit the vines that round the thatch-eves
    run."
                             —*John Keats.*

THE BOY:
*"They said, 'Now, Master Dick,
   You go to sleep right quick,
Or you'll have a goblin coming after you!'
She thought that I'd be frighted,
   But I wasn't, just excited,
And I hardly could believe it might be true.
Then she went down the stair
   And I said an extra prayer:
'Oh, please, do let me see that goblin, do!'"

THE GIRL:
 "He could tell us lots of things
   About fairy queens and kings,
And playful Puck and all his merry band,
And all about the gnomes,
   And about the fairy homes,
And the pixies with their elfin mischief,
   And —
Best of all he'd add
   If we are very bad,
He'd take us with him off to Goblin Land."

JACK-O'-LANTERN (*appears without his lantern*):
 "We've cut our wheat and we've brought it in,
   The golden grain is in the bin.
   Our work was hard, but work will win.
   Hurrah for Harvest Home!

 "Potatoes deep in the cellar lie,
   And yellow pumpkins that make good pie,

---

* By I. T. Mills.   Copyright, "Child Education," Evans Bros., London.

And apples stored in the attic high.
Hurrah for Harvest Home!"
                                                    —*Laurence Hutton.*

A GOBLIN (*leading one of the black cats*):
        "Pixie, kobold, elf and sprite
        All are on their rounds tonight,
        In the wan moon's silver ray
        Thrives their helter, skelter play."

(*The* WITCH *and* SCARECROW *appear. Together, they draw back the curtain disclosing the stage.*)

SCENE I

(*Late afternoon of Hallowe'en.* OCTOBER *is seen flitting among the harvest piles and holding up one fruit and vegetable after another to see if they are perfect.* JACK-O'-LANTERN *kneels beside the pumpkins.*)

OCTOBER (*runs to* JACK *and taps him lightly*): A penny for your thoughts, Jack! What makes you look so glum on Hallowe'en? Don't you know that this is the festival of Harvest Home when the whole world rejoices in autumn's gifts of food for the year? (*She hums lightly.*)

        Peter, Peter, Pumpkin Eater,
        Had a wife and couldn't keep her.
        Put her in a pumpkin shell,
        And there he kept her very well.

Is that what you are thinking about, my dear?

JACK-O'-LANTERN: You are just like everyone else, October, thinking only of my cousin, Peter, and not of me. I wish I had been given some other vegetable for my own. Ever since I can remember, Peter's pumpkin house and Cinderella's pumpkin coach have been talked about in the family. No one has a good word to say about me.

OCTOBER: Fie, Jack! Don't you know the reason for that? Peter built himself a pumpkin house, and

Cinderella's coach helped to make her a princess. If you want to attract attention to yourself, Jack, you must do something to make your family proud of you. Only see the important place I have made for myself in the company of the months just by learning how to paint apples and leaves better than any of them. Do something! Don't dream about it under the shadow of the corn shocks.

JACK: What can I do, October? (*The* BOY *and* GIRL *are seen approaching. They stop at the gate, talking to one another.*)

OCTOBER: Hush! Here come two mortals! They must not see us!

JACK-O'-LANTERN: Where shall I hide?

OCTOBER: Cover yourself with one of these pumpkins. Come with me!
(JACK *lifts and holds one of the pumpkins in front of himself as he and* OCTOBER *exit. The* BOY *and* GIRL *enter through the gate.*)

THE BOY: *Two* pumpkins did you say, Sister?

THE GIRL: Yes, two. We children have such enormous appetites that Mother says she shall have to make at least four pumpkin pies to last over Sunday.

THE BOY: I don't feel like carrying home two pumpkins, and the apples, and the potatoes, and the corn.

THE GIRL (*severely and shaking her finger at him*): And you didn't feel like wiping the dinner dishes for me, or going to the store, or taking care of the baby. You forgot to feed the chickens. Is that the way for a boy to behave? What do the stories say about goblins at this time of the year? Tonight, you know, will be Hallowe'en.

THE BOY: "The goblins will get me if I don't watch out." (*Laughs.*) There are no goblins. (*A tiny laugh is heard off-stage. The* BOY *starts.*) Did you hear someone laughing, Sister?

THE GIRL (*peers about in all the corners of the stage*): I thought I did. I have known people, very old people, who said they had seen goblins on Hallowe'en. They come out to play tricks on mortals and if a child has not been kind during the year they take him away. Now pick two pumpkins and help me carry them home.

(*The* BOY *crosses to where the remaining pumpkin is and looks surprised.*)

THE BOY: There were two pumpkins growing here in the garden, I am very sure. I have seen them getting larger all summer. Now there is only one.

THE GIRL: Perhaps you can find the other pumpkin. We must have two for those pies.

(*She gathers vegetables from the garden, filling a basket she carries on her arm.*)

THE BOY (*sits down on the ground and eats an apple*): This is the best time of the whole year, with so many good things to eat: nuts, apples, pears, corn to pop, pumpkin pies—

THE GIRL (*shakes the* BOY *a little*): Can't you do anything to help me? Then let us go home. I think it is growing dark already, and strange things happen on Hallowe'en.

(*She picks the pumpkin and tugs it, together with her full basket, out through the gate. The* BOY *follows. As they exit there is a chorus of* GOBLIN *laughter off-stage. They both look back fearfully.*)

SCENE II

Hallowe'en

(*The stage is dark, but slowly lightens as if the moon were rising. The musicians play elfin music as, one by one, the* GOBLINS *appear from behind the corn shocks. They dance in time to the music grotesquely. At the end of their dance they scatter about the stage, some playing toss and catch with the apples and vegetables, others gathering together in groups to whisper and chuckle.*)

FIRST GOBLIN:

>Morning and evening
>Maids hear the goblins cry:
>"Come buy our orchard fruits,
>Come buy.   Come buy

SECOND GOBLIN:

>Apples and quinces,
>Lemons and oranges,
>Plump unpecked cherries,
>Melons and raspberries,

THIRD GOBLIN:

>Bloom-down-cheeked peaches,
>Swart-headed mulberries,
>Wild free-born cranberries,
>Crab apples, dewberries,

FOURTH GOBLIN:

>Pineapples, blackberries,
>Apricots, strawberries,
>All ripe together
>In summer weather."   —*Christina Rossetti*

(*The* GOBLINS *select fruits from their sacks and taste them.*)

FIRST GOBLIN: Our harvest is in.

SECOND GOBLIN: Now, fun shall begin!

THIRD GOBLIN: Each Hallowe'en sprite.

FOURTH GOBLIN: Makes merry tonight.

(*The* BLACK CATS *appear, scamper about the stage, and then join the* GOBLINS *in a circle. They play a simple game of tag, in and out of the circle, in time to running music. The* SCARECROW *and the* WITCH *enter, arm in arm, talking earnestly. The* GOBLINS *and* BLACK CATS *surround them, listening. The* SCARECROW *carries* BOY'S *trousers. The* WITCH *has his jacket.*)

SCARECROW: If I had as fine a pair of trousers as these, you would never find me standing in a corn-field all summer to frighten the crows. I should be going to school, and helping with the chores when I came home in the afternoon.

THE WITCH: The boy who wore this jacket would be just the right size to ride over the forest on the end of my broomstick. I need a pilot, riding about alone as I must. The sky traffic is dangerous now, because of the airships.

THE GOBLINS (*all together*): A mortal's clothes!

FIRST GOBLIN: The mortal's a child.

SECOND GOBLIN: And sure to be wild!

THIRD GOBLIN: He'll look for his jacket.

FOURTH GOBLIN: Then, ho, for a racket!

THE SCARECROW: Where did you find that little jacket, Madam Witch?

WITCH: With its sleeves caught to the points of the new moon. The Boy must be off for a journey. Where, if I may ask, did you discover those trousers?

SCARECROW: Astride the Little Bear in the Hallowe'en Sky. They fell down into my field. I believe I know their Boy.

WITCH: We must find him.

SCARECROW: And give him his clothes. (*They exit.*)

FIRST GOBLIN: The mortal's asleep!

Second Goblin: In Goblin Land deep!

Third Goblin: Let's give him his due.

Fourth Goblin: His dream shall come true.

(Scarecrow *and* Witch *enter with the* Boy *between them, dressed, and rubbing the sleep from his eyes. He is frightened as the* Goblins *crowd around him, poking and pinching him playfully.*)

First Goblin: A child who won't work—

Second Goblin: Inclining to shirk.

Third Goblin: We shall spirit away.

Fourth Goblin: For work, and no play!

(October *and the* Girl *enter, leading* Jack-o'-Lantern *between them;* Jack *carries a lighted pumpkin lantern, which seems to diffuse a light over the entire stage. At sight of this, the* Goblins *disperse and huddle in groups among the* Black Cats.)

The Girl: I came for my brother. (*Puts her arms protectingly about him.*)

Jack: I brought him a light.

The Girl: He dreamed about goblins.

Jack: That come in the night.

The Girl: He's sure to be good now.

October: As helpful as you. (*Beckons to the* Goblins.) Come, empty your bundles, and show what you do.

(*The* Goblins *show their fruits and vegetables, dancing about with them held high for the children to see, and then laying them in a pile at the* Boy's *feet.* October *leads.*)

Jack (*comes to the front of the stage; holds his lantern high*):
A light for the children on Hallowe'en night,
Turns mischief to frolic, and darkness to light!

(*The* Goblins *crowd around* Jack-o'-Lantern, *inspecting his lantern and nodding their heads to agree with him. Then each selects a* Black Cat *for a partner.* Jack-o'-Lantern, *with* October *as his partner, leads the* PLAYERS *in a grand march.   Behind him come the* BOY *and* GIRL, SCARECROW *and* WITCH *and last the* GOBLINS *with the* BLACK CATS.)

SUGGESTED MUSIC FOR THE PLAY

"English Harvesters Dance"... *The Folk Dance Book, Crampton*
"Nixie Polka"............... *The Folk Dance Book, Crampton*
"Dance of the Gnomes"......................... *Reinhold*
"The Elves"... *Grieg*
"In the Hall of the Mountain King".................... *Grieg*
"Witch's Dance"............................. *MacDowell*
"Hansel and Gretel"......................... *Humperdinck*
"Babes in Toyland March"....................... *Herbert*
"Money Musk" ....
    Rhythms and Dances for Elementary Schools, La Salle

Tabby's Thanksgiving Doll
By Rebecca Rice

THE PLAYERS

TABBY—A Little Girl.
PATTY—The Older Sister.
JOHN—A Brother.
PETER—Another Brother.
WETONAH—An Indian Girl of Tabby's Age.
WABEEK—Wetonah's Brother.
MOTHER.

TIME—The Week before Thanksgiving.

PLACE—A Colonial Kitchen.

TABBY'S THANKSGIVING DOLL

By Rebecca Rice

COSTUMES

The children are dressed in sober grays, blues and browns. The girls wear little white caps, white aprons and buckles on their shoes. Their skirts nearly touch the floor. Tabby is much smaller than Patty. The boys wear collars and cuffs of white. Their shoe-buckles are larger than those worn by the girls. The making of large paper collars, cardboard buckles silvered with paint, and paper caps and aprons is a worth-while problem for the class.

The Indian children wear either the regulation Indian play suits or brown denim, beaded, with headbands of bright crepe-paper feathers. Without a doubt good costumes add to the effectiveness of any play, and if it is practical these might be planned from actual photographs of old paintings found in museums and libraries. It is equally true that the mere suggestion of dress satisfies children. This play may be put on with very little trouble as to costuming.

THE PLAY

(*The scene is laid in a Colonial kitchen. At the middle back of the stage is a large fireplace. Left of the fireplace is a small chair or hassock and a doll's cradle patterned after an old-fashioned wooden cradle. At the right of the stage is a table with apples, bowls, raisins and knives upon it.* TABBY *is sitting in the little chair, a corncob doll on her lap. There is a window at the right of the fireplace with a curtain. The action takes place without the players looking toward this window.*)

TABBY (*kissing her corncob doll fondly*): You are my own dear baby. Your name is Constance, for that is the prettiest name I know. (*She wraps a little shawl about Constance and begins to rock her in her arms.*) Hush-a-by, hush-a-by. It is your bedtime, dear, and I will sing to you. (*She sings a lullaby.*) There, my baby is asleep. (PATTY *enters, hiding something under her apron.*

TABBY *puts finger to her lips.*)   Sh, do not wake my baby. Such a time as I have had getting her to sleep. (*She lays the doll down in the cradle not noticing that* PATTY *is hiding something.* PATTY *slips into a chair at the table, but keeps one hand in her lap.*)

PATTY: I will be as quiet as a little gray mouse. I would not wake your baby for anything.   Mother says it makes babies cross to wake them.
(*A dark hand moves the curtains apart as if someone were looking into the kitchen from the forest outside.   There is a faint whistle like that of a bird.* PATTY *starts, and the hand is withdrawn.*)

TABBY: What was that?

PATTY: I don't know.   Oh, here come mother and John.   That's who it was.
(MOTHER *and* JOHN *enter at one side.* MOTHER *crosses to table and sits down.*)

TABBY: Sh, do not wake my baby.

MOTHER: No, indeed.

JOHN (*rather loudly and with all a boy's scorn*): Pooh, 'tis nothing but a corncob, and even if it were a real puppet from old England, it could not go to sleep. Before I'd be so silly over an old puppet!   What a baby you are!

TABBY (*nearly crying*): I am not a baby, John Bradley.   I am five years old! And 'tis not a silly puppet.   'Tis my baby.   Look, you have awakened her.   (*She takes Constance up and hugs her.*)

JOHN: Of all the silly—

MOTHER: Hush, John.   Let the child alone.   You are too big to tease her so.   Besides there is much work for all of us if we are to be ready for Thanksgiving.   I have these apples to peel and pies to make. (*She starts to peel apples.*)   Where is Peter?

JOHN: He took grain to the grist mill. He remembered that you said there was hardly enough flour in the barrel to make all the plum puddings and pies for Thanksgiving.

PATTY: I was with Peter when he went to the attic for nuts, and what do you suppose we found?

JOHN: I cannot guess.

PATTY: Some bad squirrels had come in through a small hole and had carried away a great many nuts.

TABBY (*coming close to her sister's side*): Won't we have enough nuts for Thanksgiving?

PATTY: We will have all we want, for Peter followed Master Squirrel to his hollow tree and found even more nuts than had been stolen.

MOTHER: Did he take them all?

PATTY: No, Mother. He said that they were the squirrel's winter store, and without them he would starve. Peter said that he remembers how hungry you were the first winter you came to live in the Massachusetts Bay Colony although he was only a little boy then, and he wouldn't make a squirrel suffer so.

PETER (*entering from the right and walking toward center of stage*): Here is a bag of fine flour and here are the nuts for your cake, Mother. (TABBY *goes to meet him and takes a handful of nuts.*) Get out of that dish, Tabby Bradley. I did not crack those butternuts for little girls to eat. I cracked them for our Thanksgiving dinner. (*He sits down at the table next to his mother.*)

PATTY (*rubbing her stomach*): Mm, nice fruity pies and plum puddings. (*She counts the pies on her fingers as she mentions them.*) Mince pie, apple pie, squash pie and pumpkin pie, all criss-crossed with bars of crust. My, how busy our big brick oven will be from now until Thanksgiving.

JOHN (*sniffing*): I like Thanksgiving. There are so many smells and tastes in the kitchen. (*He walks over to the table and helps himself to a quarter of an apple, then brings one to* TABBY.) Who is going to stone raisins?

PATTY: Did anyone say raisins? It is my turn to stone them because Tabby did it last time. (PATTY *leans over and picks up a sticky mass of raisins from the table, eating a few; then she leans over and helps herself to a nut.* PETER *puts both hands over the nut bowl.*)

PETER: Mother, Patty is in the nuts now. There won't be one left for Thanksgiving dinner. These girls are worse than the squirrels!

(*The window curtains part again and the face of an Indian boy appears. He reaches in as far as he dares, looking all about. Then he draws back, with a slight scratching sound as he climbs down.*)

JOHN: What was that?

PETER (*going to window and looking out*): Just the squirrel, John, who wants our nuts; I hear him scampering through the leaves.

MOTHER (*trying to hide her anxiety, as she also looks out of the window*): Of course it was only a squirrel, children. How glad we shall be to have your father home from his hunting for Thanksgiving!

PATTY (*holds up raisin*): Here is a raisin for a good little girl.

TABBY (*going for the raisin*): I am a good girl. And now I shall take Constance out for she needs some air. (*She kneels down beside the cradle, wraps Constance up and starts for the door. Again the curtains flutter and the whistle sounds in the forest.*)

JOHN: Wait a bit, Tabby. I'll go with you. I've got to feed the pigs. (*He gets pail.*) Look, you can put your puppet on your back, Indianwise, and I will hold your hand.

TABBY: Yes, I will hold your hand and give Constance a ride. (*She puts the puppet in the shawl over her shoulder and they go off at the right.*)

PATTY (*follows them to the door, something still hidden under her apron*): I am glad Tabby is gone. Now I can finish the puppet I am making for her. (*She takes a small rag doll from under her apron and sits down in the little chair where* TABBY *had been. She holds the doll up.*) Look, don't you think she has a pretty face?

MOTHER (*goes over to examine doll*): It is a lovely puppet, and it was kind of you to make it for Tabby.

PATTY: I like to make puppets, but I am too old to play with them myself. I like its cunning little hood and apron. I stuffed the head with a bit of wool. Then I stretched a piece of white linen over the knob of wool and tied it tightly about the neck.

PETER: How did you make the face?

PATTY: I drew it on the linen with a piece of charcoal and went over the marks with the colored thread I use on my sampler. I made the face pink with the juice of berries.

MOTHER: Let me see it, Patty. (PATTY *carries the doll to her mother who examines it closely.*) Those are nice little stitches. It pleases me when you take pains. It is almost finished, isn't it?

PATTY (*going back to the seat near the cradle*): There are only a few more stitches to sew this string in place. Look, now it is done.

PETER: Tabby will be glad that you made the dress blue like her own new one. She likes the new one Mother spun, wove and made for her so well.

PATTY (*cuddling doll*): It was the prettiest shade of blue mother ever made. I want my next dress the same color. Do you know, I am sorry this puppet is done. I have had such a good time making it.

MOTHER: After Thanksgiving I will make you some cloth and let you stitch it into a dress for yourself.

PATTY: Oh, Mother! (*She holds up her finger.*) What is that? (*A sound of crying is heard.*)

MOTHER: It is Tabby crying. I wonder if she is hurt. Something serious must have happened. (TABBY's *voice is heard in loud wails.* JOHN's *voice is heard before they enter.*)

JOHN: Aw, Tabby, don't cry. 'Twould never have happened if I had been right there. (*They enter.* TABBY *is digging her fists into her eyes while* JOHN *regards her with sympathy.*)

MOTHER (*going to* TABBY *and putting her arms about her*): What is the matter, dear? Tell mother.

TABBY: My baby, oh, my baby!

PATTY: What happened? Tell us, Tabby. (TABBY *sobs something into the corner of her apron which no one understands.*)

MOTHER (*to* JOHN, *who is beginning to rub his sleeve over his eyes*): John, did you hurt you little sister?

JOHN: No. I didn't do anything at all. I was in the barn getting food for the pig and Tabby was waiting outside for me. She screamed and I ran out to see what was the matter. I saw an Indian boy running toward the wood with something in his hand.

TABBY: My baby, oh, my baby!

PETER: Come on, John. Let's follow him. Perhaps we can get the puppet back. (*They run out.*)

MOTHER: Be careful, boys! I don't think you had better. (PATTY *goes to door.*)

PATTY: It's no use. They have gone. They probably won't catch the boy anyway, for Indians go so fast. Don't cry so, Tabby (*holding out the new rag doll*). See, Tabby, I have made a new puppet for you.

TABBY: I want my baby. I want Constance. (*She looks at new doll and takes it in her hands.*) It is very pretty. (*Her voice breaks.*) But it isn't Constance. (*She sits on stool with the new rag doll held listlessly on her lap.*) I didn't see him coming, till he was right beside me and he took her right out of my arms and ran away. He will scalp her and burn her at the stake. (*She sits there sobbing softly. The mother goes back to her work.* PATTY *goes to the window.*)

PATTY: Oh, come quick! The boys have got the Indian boy and are almost carrying him. There is a little Indian girl there, too.

TABBY: Have they got Constance?

PATTY: I can't see her. The little girl is crying. (*The boys enter, dragging an Indian boy with them. He has hurt his ankle and they are half carrying him. A little Indian girl comes also, looking as unhappy as* TABBY.)

PETER: Well, we caught your thief, Tabby, but we wouldn't have caught him if he had not twisted his ankle and sprained or broken it. I brought him home, Mother, for I knew that you'd fix him up. (*The mother examines the hurt Indian boy.*)

MOTHER: 'Tis a sprain. I will bind it up. Get linen strips from the chest, Patty. (*The little Indian girl and* TABBY *are in the middle of the room.*

*Constance is in the little Indian girl's arms.   The new doll is on
the stool.*)

TABBY: That is my baby. It is my Constance.
(*She holds out her hands for it.   The Indian child holds it tighter.*)

WETONAH: No.

TABBY: Yes.   Give it to me!

WETONAH: No.
(TABBY *takes the corncob doll from her by force.   WETONAH
drops down on the floor and bursts into a loud wail.   TABBY looks
down at her uncertainly, her own lip quivering.   Others watch
them.*)

WABEEK (*Indian boy*): She never had one.   (*He
points to puppet.*)

TABBY: Never had a puppet?

PATTY: The poor little thing!   I'll—

TABBY (*running to* PATTY *and putting her arms about her*):
Patty, would you cry if I gave away my pretty new
puppet?

PATTY: Of course not.   I'd be glad.
(TABBY *gets the rag doll and going down on her knees beside*
WETONAH, *puts her arm about her and the doll into her arms.*)

TABBY: That is for you.   It is a lovely puppet
my sister made me.   (WETONAH *hugs new doll and looks
up with a radiant smile.*)

WETONAH: Pretty, pretty!   You good! (*She shows
puppet to* WABEEK *whose sullen expression changes to a pleased
one.*)

PATTY (*with deep satisfaction*):   I like to make puppets.
Now I can make Tabby another one.

TABBY (*including all in a satisfied smile and with Constance
held close*): I am thankful now!

WETONAH (*hugging the rag doll*):   Thankful now!

The Home-Coming

By Winifred E. Howe and Carolyn Sherwin Bailey

THE PLAYERS

DONALD—A Boy of Today.

DOROTHY—Donald's Sister.

THE SPIRIT OF LONG AGO—A Tall Child.

PARSON CAPEN—An Older Boy.

PRISCILLA CAPEN, The Parson's Wife—An Older Girl.

ELIZABETH BRADSTREET, The Parson's Daughter—A Motherly Girl.

SIMON BRADSTREET, Elizabeth's Husband—A Soldierly Boy.

BETTY BRADSTREET—A Very Small, Plump Child.

THE BRADSTREET BABY, named for his Father—A Big Doll.

A COMPANY OF PURITANS—Boys Who are Straight and Can March Well.

AN INDIAN—A Dark Boy.

THE HOME-COMING

By Winifred E. Howe and Carolyn Sherwin Bailey

THE COSTUMES

Donald and Dorothy wear their everyday clothes except that Donald's knee breeches are black and both have white stockings. In Scene II, the Spirit of Long Ago gives Dorothy a long, full dress of pretty figured goods, white with dainty sprays of pink and blue, a white kerchief and cuffs, and a close-fitting embroidered muslin cap. She gives Donald a coat with a fall of lace at the neck and wrists and a white satin waistcoat. These period clothes are put on over their everyday ones. She gives them also low shoes with big silvered buckles. The Spirit of Long Ago is dressed in the costume of the Puritans, a dark gray dress of homespun made long and full, a generous apron of white linen falling almost to the floor, a large kerchief, snowy white, crossed on her breast, white cuffs turned back on her long sleeves, and a white cap covering her dark hair which is drawn back smoothly. Parson Capen and his family are dressed in Puritan costume, but as if they were indoors keeping Thanksgiving Day. Elizabeth Bradstreet wears a long dress of blue calico, cap and apron. Simon Bradstreet wears the uniform of a Colonial soldier. Little Betty is amusingly costumed exactly as Dorothy is. The doll wears a long baby's slip of ruffled, embroidered muslin with short sleeves. Parson Capen and Priscilla will need white wigs. The Company of Puritans wear black suits, deep collars and cuffs of white, hats with tall crowns and wide brims, and low square-toed shoes. One of the Company is a drummer. The Indian wears moccasins, a bright blanket and many feathers.

STAGE DIRECTIONS

A large and forbidding door is painted in the center of a drop curtain or on a screen framework which stands at the front of the stage. Across the top are six small insets of glass. Below are stout wooden panels. To the right and left are pillars carved in a design of stiff leaves. It has a large black latch.

The floor of the stage is bare. The walls are hung with some coarse stuff that will give the effect of rough plastering. There is a fireplace at the back which may, if necessary, be painted on a screen. It has andirons, a crane with hanging pots and a tea-kettle. Small diamond-paned windows are indicated, and an old portrait or two are hung on the wall. On one side of the room is a staircase. This may be arranged by draping wooden boxes or a stepladder. On the other side is an old-fashioned chest. Other stage furnishings are a wooden settle, an old-fashioned wooden cradle, a rush-bottomed chair, a plain table, and a chest of drawers upon which are blue and white dishes, pewter or tin plates, and a brass candlestick of Colonial design. There are exits at right and left.

Accessory stage furnishings include a very large Bible with clasps, a flax wheel, a goose quill pen, quaint inkstand and sand sifter, a tall clock, and a cat if one can be persuaded to take part in the play. Otherwise a toy cat may bask in front of the fire.

SCENE I

Twilight of the Day before Thanksgiving

DONALD (*holding* DOROTHY'S *hand as the two children stand in front of the door*): What an odd door! Just like the ones Father showed us in New England. He said a door like this could stand the buffeting of the winds and the beating of the rain for two hundred years.

DOROTHY (*clapping her hands softly*): Let's play it is as old as that. I never saw it here before. Shall we play Puritans here, all by ourselves?

DONALD: Right! We will. You and I have been having adventures together ever since we could walk, Mother says. We'll go through this old door, Dorothy, and find out what there is behind it.

(*The children tug at the latch and push against the lower panels, but the door does not move.* DONALD *raises his fist and knocks loudly three times. Rap, rap, rap; the sound is repeated back-stage like an echo. A minute passes—it seems an hour—then far away they hear a light tap, tap, a regular footfall growing steadily louder and louder, and at last the grating of a heavy key in a keyhole, a sharp click as the latch is lifted, and a rasping note as if the door were opened a crack. As the door opens wide, the children see the* Spirit of Long Ago. *Her candle, held high in one hand, throws a flickering ray of light upon the upturned faces of* Donald *and* Dorothy.)

The Spirit of Long Ago: What do you want, children? (*Her voice and smile are welcoming.*)

Donald: We were just saying we should like to play Puritan.

The Spirit of Long Ago: Not tonight. Did you not know that this is the very night when all your forefathers from north and south, and from east and west, return here to visit their old homes?

Dorothy (*so eager that she forgets to be afraid*): Then we want more than ever to come in.

Donald: Indeed we do!

The Spirit of Long Ago (*after considering for a moment*): I believe I will let you come in to my party if you will be very quiet. Children of my time were seen, but not heard, you know.

(*The stage is darkened for a brief space except for the candle's light to indicate the vanishing of nearly two hundred years. This allows for the removal of the door. The stage reappears dimly at first, and then as in the light of a Colonial kitchen.*)

SCENE II

Parson Capen's Home in Topsfield, Connecticut

(Donald *and* Dorothy *are seen running about the room on tip-toe, pinching themselves to be sure they are not dreaming. They try the chair and settle, smooth the cat and rock the wooden cradle.*)

The Spirit of Long Ago (*watching the children and*

laughing): You funny children! Where have you come from? Where did you find those strange clothes? Little Betty Bradstreet, who will be here soon, must find you properly dressed.

(*She kneels in front of the chest, as* DONALD *and* DOROTHY *peer over her shoulder, opens it, and takes out old-fashioned suits and dresses, hats and caps and shoes, homespun linens and quilts. The children hold the garments up to themselves and carry out the pantomime of trying them on. Finally the* SPIRIT *selects costumes for the children and lays away the others.*)

THE SPIRIT OF LONG AGO (*holding out* DONALD'S *buckled shoes, ruffled coat and satin waistcoat*): For you. A boy of the Colonies you will soon become. (*On her other arm is* DOROTHY'S *figured dress and cap.*) When you, little girl, put on these dainty clothes, you too will belong with your forefathers.

(DONALD *and* DOROTHY *costume themselves, and look at each other in amazement. Gradually, feeling the dignity of the dress, they become more sober.* DONALD *bows and* DOROTHY *drops a curtsy, as the two clasp hands and dance the minuet.*)

THE SPIRIT OF LONG AGO: That is surely better. Now I must write my Thanksgiving proclamation. Bring me the silver inkstand from the top of our chest of drawers, and bring also the sand shaker to dry the ink. I have paper here and a new pen cut from a goose-quill.

(*Both children start to run for the writing materials, but it is* DONALD *who brings them, because* DOROTHY *trips on the long skirt to which she is unaccustomed. They find the* SPIRIT *seated at the table, her paper spread out before her, the candlelight dancing over it. Dipping the quill pen in the ink, she writes carefully as the children watch her. They read a word or a sentence aloud from time to time. As a page is filled the* SPIRIT *pours grains of sand over it from the shaker. When the writing is finished* DOROTHY, *walking slowly, returns the inkstand, shaker and pen to the chest of drawers. Waving the proclamation with a satisfied flourish, the* SPIRIT *reads it aloud.*)

THANKSGIVING PROCLAMATION
* General Court of the Connecticut Colony, October 23rd, 1676

This Court, considering the enlarged goodness of God to His people in this wilderness in appearing so gloriously for their help in subduing of enemies in so good a measure as He hath done, and His mercy in removing sickness from the land, in the comfortable and plentiful harvest that we have received, and the continuance of our privileges and liberties, civil and ecclesiastical, has been moved to nominate and appoint the first day of November to be solemnly kept a day of Thanksgiving throughout this Colony to bless and praise the Lord for His great mercy toward us; and with prayers that the Lord will help us in our lives and ways to walk answerable to His abundant mercies.

(*Folding the sheet neatly and fastening it with a wafer, the* SPIRIT *claps her hands, and instantly before the astonished eyes of the children there enters a small company of Puritan men. Two by two, led by one beating upon a drum, the men march up to the* SPIRIT, *then stop with military precision. The captain steps forward and receives the proclamation, the line wheels, and before the children can recover their breath the procession exits.*

DONALD *starts to whistle, then looks at his clothes and stops.* DOROTHY *still stares at the exit.*)

DOROTHY: They were like the picture in our history!

DONALD: I wonder where they have taken the Thanksgiving proclamation.

(*The* SPIRIT *smiles and puts her finger to her lips. Then she swiftly lights the fire in the fireplace and straightens a cushion here, a chair there, and sets the table for a meal with housewifely deftness as if guests were expected. She motions to the children to seat themselves in the dimness of the stairway as if they were hidden near the attic. Last, she winds the clock, which begins to tick loudly.*)

*This is the first recorded Thanksgiving Proclamation of the American people.

THE SPIRIT OF LONG AGO: Now watch, children.
The party will soon begin.

SCENE III

The Home-Coming

(*The children are seated high on the staircase, the* SPIRIT OF
LONG AGO *close to them in the shadows and pointing toward the
entrance on the other side of the stage. Distant voices are heard
off-stage. A board creaks.* PARSON CAPEN *enters, looking about
as if he were dreaming and rubbing the sleep from his eyes.*)

THE SPIRIT OF LONG AGO (*speaking softly*): That is
dear old Parson Capen of Topsfield. I knew he
would come. The one place in the world he wants
to find is a room just like his old kitchen in New
England.

(PARSON CAPEN *reaches the center of the room and gives a cry
of pleasure. He beckons toward the entrance.* PRISCILLA CAPEN,
ELIZABETH *and* SIMON BRADSTREET *and* BETTY *enter.* ELIZABETH
carries the baby carefully in her arms, and BETTY *holds tightly to
her father's coat tails.*)

THE SPIRIT OF LONG AGO: Here come Priscilla,
Parson Capen's wife, and Elizabeth, his daughter,
with her husband, Simon Bradstreet. There are the
Bradstreet children, Betty, and Simon, the baby.
They have all come home to keep Thanksgiving.

(PARSON CAPEN *seats himself beside the wide brick fireplace
and stretches out his hands to its welcome heat. His daughter,
knowing his wants, brings him from a chest of drawers a large
Bible of leather with heavy clasps, and he soon is absorbed in reading
by the flickering light.* PRISCILLA *examines everything in the
familiar room,—the fireplace with its pots and teakettle, and large
andirons; the oven at the back; the settle, narrow of seat but with
a back high enough to form a shield from the chilly draught; the
table with its plates and bowls. She traces with a finger the lines
of the rude carving upon the chest of drawers, then opens the drawers
and counts the spotless napkins and tablecloths within, home-spun
and home-woven, her handiwork. She stoops over the cradle,*

rocking it slightly and dreaming for a moment. She lifts a pewter platter that came across the ocean from England, the home of her ancestors. At last she settles, satisfied, in a chair by the fire and listens to the friendly ticking of the clock.

ELIZABETH BRADSTREET *places little* SIMON *in the cradle.* BETTY *sits on the floor leaning against her grandfather's knee and playing with the cat upon the hearth. A friendly* INDIAN *enters and joins the group, standing silent and motionless by the fire.)*

DONALD: They don't see us at all.

THE SPIRIT OF LONG AGO: But you see them.

DOROTHY: How happy they are to be at home.

THE SPIRIT OF LONG AGO: Ah, yes; at home in your hearts.

DONALD: Why don't they speak?

THE SPIRIT OF LONG AGO: The voices of our fore-fathers speak to children every Thanksgiving Day. *(She exits mysteriously without the children seeing her go.)*

(DONALD and DOROTHY come down from the stairway and join the group about the hearth. The home people are not aware of their presence. DOROTHY kneels beside the cradle and rocks it. DONALD stands beside SIMON BRADSTREET, stretching up as he tries to be as tall as this Colonial soldier.)

MOTHER'S VOICE *(this is a voice heard off-stage)*: Donald, Dorothy!
(The PURITANS *start. They exit one at a time and silently, leaving the children alone.)*

MOTHER'S VOICE: Children, wake up! It is Thanksgiving Day.
(The children seem to awaken from a dream. If desired, all the PLAYERS *may return and group themselves for a final tableau with* DONALD *and* DOROTHY *about the Thanksgiving table.)*

The Three Trees

By Gertrude Maynard

THE PLAYERS

LARGE TREE—A Larger Child.
MIDDLE-SIZED TREE—A Smaller Child.
LITTLE TREE—A Very Small Child.
JACK FROST.
NORTH WIND.
RABBIT.
CHRISTMAS FAIRY.
SANTA CLAUS.
CHRISTMAS MOTHER.

THE THREE TREES

By GERTRUDE MAYNARD

SCENE I—*In the Forest, Christmas Eve.*
SCENE II—*As for Scene I.*

STAGE DIRECTIONS

Lay white sheets loosely on the floor space selected for the stage and sprinkle with star dust and bits of silver tinsel. Near the center front place three Christmas trees of graded heights. The standards of the trees should be covered by evergreen branches and trailing pine to preserve the realism of the forest setting. A child costumed in green or white stands behind each tree. Little Tree is as tiny a child as possible who is able to speak the lines. The smallest tree which conceals this child is placed under or near electric attachments for lighting it, and these lights are in readiness for immediate use. There is an entrance from the side either by screen or door. It is desirable to have a father or an older brother for Santa Claus. There is a real mother.

A few understudies are arranged for by a listening group of children at rehearsals. These children learn the dialogue and action unconsciously and can be depended upon to help out in the emergency which so often arises when putting on a play with young children.

There is descriptive music throughout, either piano or phonograph.

Scene I opens with quiet music.

SCENE I

When the Forest has Become Dark

BIG TREE: It is going to be a cold night.

MIDDLE-SIZED TREE: Yes, I feel the cold in my very roots. It is just the kind of a night that Santa Claus loves.

LITTLE TREE: Are you sure Santa Claus is coming tonight?

BIG TREE: Yes, it is Christmas Eve. He will come through the forest very soon.

LITTLE TREE: I suppose you will be taken for a Christmas tree.

BIG TREE: I hope so. I am certainly a fine large tree, the very largest tree in this part of the forest.

MIDDLE-SIZED TREE: I think myself that you are a little too large. Now I am about the right size, neither too large nor too small.

LITTLE TREE (*sighing*): I shall have to wait for years before I shall be big enough to be a Christmas tree.

BIG TREE: Yes, my dear, it will be at least five years before Santa Claus will even look at you.

MIDDLE-SIZED TREE: Here comes Jack Frost! He will make it colder still.

(*Enter* JACK FROST *to the music, "The Snow is Dancing," Debussy. He is a little boy, dressed in a close-fitting, white woolen suit consisting of pull-over sweater and leggings, trimmed if desired with twisted silver paper icicles and cut-paper snow crystals. He dances about and recites an old poem.*)

JACK FROST:
Oh, I am Jack Frost, a roguish little fellow.
When the winter winds begin to bellow
I fly like a little bird through the air
And creep through the little cracks everywhere.
I make little girls say, "Oh, oh, oh!"
And I make little boys say, "Ho, ho, ho!"
I pull little children by the ears

And draw from their eyes the big round tears.
I nip little children on the nose
And I pinch little children on the toes,
But when you kindle a nice warm fire,
I make my bow and hasten to retire.

Merry Christmas to you, Trees! Here is some of my frost for you.

(JACK FROST *scatters a handful of glistening frost powder over each* TREE *and runs off the stage. The* THREE TREES, *moved from side to side by the children behind, shiver and shake, are quiet again, but at the sound of wind music sway to its rhythm. Typical wind rhythms are the "Storm" from the Overture to Wagner's "Flying Dutchman," Schubert's "Erlking," and the "Storm" motif from the Overture to "William Tell.")*

(*Enter* NORTH WIND. *She is a slender, active child and wears a gray hooded cloak of some light-weight material made full enough to toss about with her motions. She puffs her cheeks and gives a simple, interpretive dance before the* TREES, *original if possible. The sound of whistling off-stage adds to the realism of this pantomime.*)

NORTH WIND:
I am the wind and I come very fast,
Through the tall woods I blow a loud blast;
Sometimes I'm soft as a sweet little child,
And I play with the flowers and am gentle and mild;
Then gusty and shrill in the winter I roar,
If you want to be quiet close window and door;
For I am the wind and I come very fast,
Through the tall woods I can blow a loud blast.

(NORTH WIND *rushes off. The* TREES *stop swaying. Quiet music is played as the* TREES *stand waiting expectantly. Then the music changes to a hopping rhythm as* RABBIT *enters.* RABBIT *is a very small boy. His costume consists of gray pajamas with feet, a little close-fitting gray cap with gray paper ears attached. He hops about the stage hesitatingly for some time. Finally he stops before* BIG TREE.)

RABBIT: Dear Tree, I cannot seem to find my

hole tonight. I am afraid that Jack Frost has closed it. I am very cold. North Wind has been chasing me. May I stay under your branches tonight?

BIG TREE: I am sorry, little Rabbit, but I expect to be taken away for a Christmas tree tonight. You will have to find some other shelter.

(RABBIT *hops to the foot of* MIDDLF-SIZED TREE.)

RABBIT: May I stay under your branches tonight? It is dreadfully cold out here in the snow.

MIDDLE-SIZED TREE: I am very sorry for you, little Rabbit, but I am not large enough to give you shelter. Besides, I am sure Santa Claus will choose me to be the Christmas tree.

(RABBIT *hops to* LITTLE TREE.)

RABBIT: Will you give me shelter, Little Tree? I am almost frozen!

LITTLE TREE (*trembling with an eagerness to help*): I am not large enough to keep out all the cold, but I want to do my best for you. Creep under my branches, little Rabbit, and snuggle as close to me as you can.

(RABBIT *creeps close to* LITTLE TREE, *cuddling up beneath the boughs. The* TREES *stand motionless. Soft Christmas music such as* "*Silent Night*" *is played.* RABBIT *sleeps.*)

SCENE II

When the Christmas Star shines upon the Forest

(*Sleigh bells are heard in the distance, soft at first, and then clearer. Brilliant galloping music announces the coming of* SANTA CLAUS *off-stage. He is heard calling to his reindeer. He shouts a final* "*Whoa.*" SANTA CLAUS *enters.*)

SANTA CLAUS: A glorious night for my business,

and here are three fine trees among which I may choose.

(SANTA CLAUS *walks about touching, measuring, considering* the TREES. *He stops before* LARGE TREE, *who rustles in excitement.*)

SANTA CLAUS (*shaking his head*): A fine tree, but the children are not using such large ones this year.

(MIDDLE-SIZED TREE *bends slightly in anticipation as* SANTA CLAUS *stops beside it.*)

SANTA CLAUS (*again shaking his head*): A beautiful tree, but a little too large for this Christmas. (*Spies* LITTLE TREE.) Ah, this is more like it! Not a bit too large. (*Catches sight of* RABBIT *asleep under* LITTLE TREE.) Well, well, what's all this? Where did you get that rabbit, Little Tree?

LITTLE TREE: He came hopping across the snow. He was very cold, and I am trying to keep him warm.

SANTA CLAUS (*to* RABBIT): Here, sir, shake. (*Shakes hands with* RABBIT.) Why didn't you go to one of the big trees for Christmas Eve?

RABBIT: They wouldn't take me, Santa Claus. They expect to be Christmas trees.

SANTA CLAUS: They do, do they? Well, perhaps they will be sometime, but not tonight. Little Tree is the one I am going to take in my sleigh, and Bunny, you are going too. I know a little boy who will love you. I don't very often get hold of a live Christmas present. Come on; hop along with me!

(*The children now step from behind the* TREES. JACK FROST *and* NORTH WIND *re-enter, and all face the audience.* RABBIT *is close to* SANTA CLAUS. *Suddenly the* CHRISTMAS FAIRY *enters.*)

CHRISTMAS FAIRY: Welcome, Little Tree! Your

time has come. Christmas Mother, where are you? We are waiting for you. (*Waves her wand.*)

(CHRISTMAS MOTHER *enters with a box or basket of gifts and ornaments which she hangs on the Christmas tree.* CHRISTMAS FAIRY *waves her wand and the tree lights are switched on. The players move to the front of the stage with* SANTA CLAUS *in front facing the audience.*)

SANTA CLAUS:

We hope you like our Christmas play.
As for myself I cannot stay,
I have much work to do, you know,
As dashing through the world I go.
But, children, like the trees, you'll find
It's always better to be kind!

(*The players and audience join in singing, "There's a Wonderful Tree," at the end of which gifts from the Christmas tree are distributed.*)

The Christmas Card

By Victor D'Amico

THE PLAYERS

ARMAND—A boy about nine or ten years of age.
DESIGN—A boy of approximately the same age as Armand.
COLOR QUEEN—An older girl.
COLORS—Little girls in two groups.

First Set: Red, Orange, Yellow.
Second Set: Red and Green.

THE CHRISTMAS CARD

By VICTOR D'AMICO

THE STORY OF THE PLAY TOLD AS A PROLOGUE

Little Armand is desirous of giving his friends something for Christmas. Since, at his age, his allowance is small he considers an inexpensive gift and decides to draw a greeting card which, though economical, will not be lacking in cheer. His desire is frustrated because of his lack of knowledge of drawing. He sits before the fire thinking, falls asleep, and awakens in Dreamland.

THE COSTUMES

Armand may wear his everyday clothes, or an artist's smock. Design wears a long, loose frock of white cotton with different decorative bands in black running around it. Each band is a design adapted from nature; a zig-zag line represents mountain ranges, flowing lines represent ripples, there are also stars and the crescent moon. The Color Queen may have a dress of tulle or thin, dyed cheesecloth that combines the colors of the rainbow so that they mingle and seem to flow together. The Colors are dressed in crepe paper or dyed cotton costumes, each of her own color.

STAGE DIRECTIONS

If the stage has a curtain, the prologue can introduce the play with curtain drawn; otherwise a screen may conceal the sleeping Armand.

At the left of the stage and toward the middle there is a chair where Armand is seen asleep. An easel and drawing board at the right are in full view of the audience. The stage hangings can be of quite modernistic design in black and white. If desired, they may be of red with a design of green wreaths or Christmas trees.

THE ACTION OF THE PLAY

ARMAND: Here it is almost Christmas and there are so many people to whom I want to give something, but what can it be? There are Daddy, and

Mother, and Sister, and Brother, and so many
friends. I should have to be Santa Claus to send all
of them gifts. Maybe just a card would do;
they would know it carried my love. Oh, but everybody buys Christmas cards. I have it! I'll draw
the cards myself!

(*Goes to the easel to begin, but hesitates.*) But how shall I
start? Why, I never made a picture before. Oh,
I wish there were somebody to help me.

DESIGN (*enters at right as if he had stepped out of the pattern
of the stage hangings*): Hello! Here I am!

ARMAND: Who are you and where did you come
from?

DESIGN: Oh, I heard you call for me, so I came
right along, you see. Is there anything I can do
for you? You are in Dreamland where wishes come
true.

ARMAND: Well, you are just in time. I am trying
to draw a Christmas card but I don't know how to
go about it.

DESIGN:
I believe that I have with me the very thing you seek.
I'll put it right up here, where you can take a peek.

(DESIGN *unrolls a large paper he carries under arm and pins it
to the easel. The paper is black with a decorative picture of a
fantastic house in white line. A good fairy-tale illustration of a
quaintly designed house will serve as a pattern for this. There
must be well-defined architecture; door, latch, lintel, and stories,
where the colors can be put on.*)

ARMAND: Oh, isn't that pretty! I like it very
much, but I don't know why. It looks like a house
but not the kind I'm used to seeing. It must be
a fairy house!

DESIGN:

My name's Design, and if you'll look you'll find me everywhere.

In everything of beauty, I surely must be there.

I slope the roof, and twist the latch, and draw an iron hinge;

And make the walls to bulge as if the snow's weight made them cringe.

ARMAND: You must be very clever. How do you think of those lovely designs? (*Points to the decorations of* DESIGN'S *garments.*)

DESIGN (*as he mentions the different designs, he touches them on his garments*):

These lines I do not make by chance, but merely do discover;

Drawing reveals no more to me than any nature lover.

Design is never here, nor there; it is everywhere:

In the ripples of the stream,

In the mountain peaks that gleam,

In the stars, the sea, the sky,

Waiting for the artist's eye.

(*Points to the symbolic design of his costume. Is about to exit.*)

ARMAND: But wait! Won't you put some color on the Christmas house for me?

DESIGN: Color comes not within my power but I will send you some of my many little kinsmen who will help you, I am sure. *Exits.*

(*Three of the little color girls,* RED, YELLOW *and* ORANGE, *enter. They carry shapes made of colored construction papers which they pin in place on the outline of the house as they finish speaking.* YELLOW *puts on the front of the house and the door latches.* RED *affixes a Christmas wreath.* ORANGE *places a door or the windows.*)

COLORS (*together*):

We are little colors three, and we make a harmony.

You can see that we are friendly, we are chosen thus
    intently.

(ORANGE, *who keeps a middle place, steps back, and* RED *and*
YELLOW *come together, joining hands.*)

RED AND YELLOW:

We alone have manners crude and are often very
    rude,
But Orange—yellow mixed with red—shows her
    sister better bred.

(*As this line is spoken* ORANGE *steps back between* RED *and*
YELLOW.)

COLORS (*together*):   We are one but there are more.

(*Exit* YELLOW *and* ORANGE. RED *remains.* GREEN *enters
carrying a shape representing a hedge which she fastens in front
of the Christmas house on the easel.* RED *and* GREEN *then clasp
hands.*)

GREEN:

Friendly colors, too, are we,
Making color harmony.
Sometimes, too intense, we part
Lest your eyes should ache and smart.

ARMAND: Can you tell me where these lovely
colors come from?

GREEN:

I cannot tell you though I try
Our Color Queen will soon come by.

(*Exit* RED *and* GREEN *from left of stage.* *Enter* COLOR QUEEN
from the right.)

COLOR QUEEN:

Oh, little boy, you wonder where we find these lovely
    things,
That, all about you, Nature from her rainbow paint
    box flings?

We dip up azure in blue buckets from the midnight
    sky;
And catch vermilion from the hills when day begins
    to die.
We woo and win the rose, and match the butterfly's
    gay wing,
And catch bright feathers from the wings of birds
    that fly in spring.
Oh, little boy who wonders, take brush in hand and
    paint
Your Christmas card, the Colors' house, with wel-
    come from the Saint.   *Exits.*

ARMAND (*reflectively*): Now I don't see how I
was so blind as to miss all these beautiful things
that Design and the Color Queen spoke of. I suppose
in Dreamland it is easier to see. Since I am in
Dreamland where all wishes come true, I wish everyone (*he dips brushes in some jars of colors that were concealed
behind the easel and paints in large letters beneath the huge Christmas card of colored paper that hangs upon the easel*) Merry
Christmas.

The Search for Santa Claus
By Carolyn Sherwin Bailey

THE PLAYERS

SISTER—A Little Girl of Today.
BROTHER—A Little Boy of Today.
THE TOY MAN—An Older Boy.
EARTH CHILDREN:
    THE CHILD FROM NORWAY—A Fair-haired Girl.
    THE CHILD FROM ENGLAND—A Rosy-cheeked Boy.
    THE CHILD FROM MEXICO—A Dark Boy.
    THE CHILD FROM HOLLAND—A Fair-haired Girl.
    THE CHILD FROM SYRIA—A Brown-eyed Girl.
CHRISTMAS NIXIES—Little Lively Boys and Girls.
SANTA CLAUS—The Older Boy who impersonated the Toy
    Man.

THE SEARCH FOR SANTA CLAUS

By CAROLYN SHERWIN BAILEY

SCENE   I—*In a Toy Shop*
SCENE   II—*In a Home Nursery*
SCENE III—*The Same as Scene II*

STAGE DIRECTIONS

The same background with a door and a window is used for all the scenes. The door should be arranged for entrances and exits. Christmas evergreens festoon the wall space and a wreath hangs in the window. Transparent paper in the window shows drifting snow, made of cut white tissue paper, falling softly outside. Scene I presents the Toy Man behind a counter on which drums, dolls, trumpets, skates, games, toy animals, in fact as many gifts as desired, are placed. Sleds, a doll's house, and a rocking horse together with larger toys stand about the stage. A Santa Claus mask hangs on the wall. Scene II is arranged with a mantelpiece and fireplace built of large blocks, two nursery beds, two children's chairs, and a table upon which a candlestick holding a lighted candle stands. Nursery pictures hang on the wall.

In Scene III the table is placed near the window to make room for the Christmas tree which occupies the center of the stage.

THE COSTUMES

Sister and Brother wear everyday clothes. In Scene II they slip a nightgown and pajamas over these. The Toy Man is dressed as a craftsman in cap and leather apron. In Scene III he wears the usual Santa Claus costume.

The Child from Norway wears a full, straight skirt of blue dyed flannelette, white wool stockings with colored clocks, a full white cotton blouse, a scarlet jacket, very short and tight fitting, and a cap of fleecy wool cut in stocking shape. This cap may match the jacket and is tied over the head with a blue ribbon.

The Child from England is dressed like the pictures of Tiny Tim or Oliver Twist. He should wear red mittens and a crimson woolen muffler wound twice about his neck.

The Child from Mexico is barefooted. He wears a khaki or brown linen overall suit over which a bright scarf is draped. His hat is a ragged brimmed sombrero.

The Child from Holland must have wooden shoes and a wide brimmed white bonnet beneath which her flaxen braids hang. She has several full skirts of contrasting bright colors, a figured guimpe or wide girdle worn over a full waist, and a large white apron.

The Child from Syria wears a one-piece garment of white cotton, straight of line, and embroidered with red, green, blue, and yellow thread. Over her dark hair a blue veil is draped. She wears no stockings, but yellow sandals.

The Christmas Nixies are dressed like brownies except that their close-fitting suits and pointed caps are scarlet. They should have long gray beards made of yarn and fastened to their caps with elastic. Their costumes are made in one piece to cover the feet. They may carry bunches of holly and have sacks of toys or ropes of greens slung over their shoulders.

SCENE I

Christmas Eve in the Toy Shop

THE TOY MAN (*moves about the shop and rearranges his stock to better advantage. Looks out of the window at the falling snow*): A fine Christmas Eve! It couldn't be better. Everything is ready and waiting. The skates are sharpened. The dolls have opened and shut their eyes and said "Mama" for a week; they are perfect. Smell the taffy! Sniff the evergreens! (*Hears a loud knocking at his door.*) Bless me! Who's that?

(*The door opens to admit* BROTHER *followed by* SISTER. *They shake snow from their coats, stamp their feet, and look with interest about the shop.*)

BROTHER (*shakes the* TOY MAN'S *hand*): Good-evening, sir. We have come to pick out our Christmas gifts.

SISTER (*drops a curtsy to the* TOY MAN): You see, sir, we wrote letters to Santa Claus giving him a list of what we wanted, but we should like to pick out the best.

BROTHER (*moves about the shop and tests a toy train, a Jack-in-the-box, and a game*): Yes, that's it; we want to be sure that we get everything we asked for, and that the things are perfect. Some toys break the day after Christmas, you know.

SISTER (*takes a large doll in her arms and rocks it*): There may be gifts in your shop we forgot to ask for. I should like this doll because she wears dancing slippers. The doll I wanted was a baby. Now, I know I must have two.

THE TOY MAN (*watches the children in surprise and rubs his forehead thoughtfully*): All right. Go ahead. Look over the stock. There isn't a better assortment in town.

BROTHER AND SISTER (BROTHER *swings up to sit on the counter.* SISTER *dances with joy.*): Thank you! Oh, we do thank you.

SISTER (*coaxingly*): Have you any of those nice Santa Claus labels?

BROTHER (*jumps down and claps his hands*): Yes, that's the idea! We could tag our gifts and then they wouldn't go to the wrong house.

THE TOY MAN (*doubtfully*): Yes. I have plenty of Santa Claus labels, but I don't know how he would feel about my giving them to you.

BROTHER AND SISTER (*snatch labels from* TOY MAN): Oh, he won't mind. Santa Claus loves us. He won't mind in the least.

(*The children proceed to select and tie Santa Claus labels to the gifts they want. It would be better if they used original dialogue here, and as much pantomime as possible in playing with the toys. At last they finish and going to the* TOY MAN *lean over the counter. The* TOY MAN *looks at them soberly.*)

SISTER: The labels are all tied on.

BROTHER: You'll see, won't you, that Santa Claus delivers the things at our house?

SISTER: You always see Santa Claus, don't you, every Christmas Eve?

TOY MAN (*goes to the window and looks out*): There he is now, ringing his Christmas bell on the curb.

(*The children run to the window and look out.*)

SISTER (*shakes her head*): Oh, no! You've made a mistake. That is only Begging Man in his red cloak asking for pennies to buy Christmas dinners for the poor.

THE TOY MAN (*puts on his spectacles*): There is Santa Claus again carrying a Christmas tree.

BROTHER: Oh, no. Excuse me, but you're all wrong. That's our own grandfather carrying home our tree. You thought he was Santa Claus because his eyes twinkle and he has white hair.

THE TOY MAN (*turns away from the window*): There's Santa Claus just behind that shadow in the corner. Look sharp; he might see you and decide to pass you by tonight.

(*The* TOY MAN'S *shadow is thrown against the Santa Claus mask which hangs upon the wall. The children look at it, but laugh.*)

SISTER (*aside*): Rather stupid I'd call this Toy Man.

BROTHER (*also aside*): Seeing things, that's what he is. Let's go.

SISTER (*curtsying*): Good-night, sir, and don't forget to have our gifts delivered.

BROTHER (*shakes the* TOY MAN'S *hand*): Good-night, sir, and thank you for attending to our very special orders.

THE TOY MAN (*opens the door for the children*): Good-night. By the way, why not watch for Santa Claus? I've known a few boys and girls who saw him. Christmas Eve's the time if you ever do catch him, you know. Good luck to you!

SCENE II

Christmas Eve in the Nursery

(BROTHER *and* SISTER, *ready for bed, hang their stockings above the fireplace. The room is dark except for the light from the candle. The children look out through the window and then jump into bed. They go to sleep. The face of* SANTA CLAUS *is seen for a moment at the window. The side of the stage near the fireplace grows gradually lighter. The children sit up in bed.*)

SISTER: See that light!

BROTHER: Don't be afraid. I'm here!

SISTER: Of course I'm not afraid, but we never saw Santa Claus, truly. It may seem too startling.

BROTHER (*boldly*): More likely to be jolly than anything else. He's probably Dad dressed up.

SISTER (*almost in tears*): Oh, I hope not. I love father, but I love Santa Claus too in a different way. I don't want them mixed. I want to see Santa Claus.

BROTHER (*sits up in bed as the door opens slowly*): Ssh! Here he comes.

(*The music of Grieg's "Spring Song" is played off-stage. The* CHILD FROM NORWAY *enters carrying a bundle of grain tied with red ribbon in her arms. She does not see* BROTHER *and* SISTER, *but lays the grain upon the window sill and returning to the center of the stage calls the birds in pantomime, whistles to them, spreads her arms and flies, and as the music ceases lays her hands in blessing on the grain as she exits.*)

SISTER (*clasps her hands in delight*): What a dear little Norwegian girl! She left a Christmas tree for the winter birds.

BROTHER: Nice little kid. Maybe she will meet Santa. Oh!—

(*The door opens and unseen carolers are heard singing "The Yule Log." The* CHILD FROM ENGLAND *enters tugging a log, which he lays in the fireplace. He may execute the pantomime of lighting the fire with flames of scarlet paper, or a red spotlight thrown on the stage will indicate the same realistically. As he hurries to exit he collides with the* CHILD FROM MEXICO, *who enters holding a stick and a plump paper bag.* BROTHER *starts to jump out of bed.*)

BROTHER: I am going to ask that English boy to stay and keep Christmas with us.

SISTER (*pulls* BROTHER *back*): Ssh. He didn't even see us. Let's watch the Mexican boy.

(*The* CHILD FROM MEXICO *suspends his bag from a string in the ceiling. Then he dances a tarantelle to suitable music, circling the bag and finally approaching close enough to break it with his stick. A shower of candies falls. The* CHILD *gathers the candies and fills the stockings. He turns to see the* CHILD FROM HOLLAND, *who has just entered, watching him. She carries a bundle of hay. He exits hurriedly. Sleigh bells off-stage indicate prancing reindeer drawing* SANTA CLAUS' *sleigh. The* CHILD FROM HOLLAND *peers up through the fireplace, then removes one of her wooden shoes and fills it with hay, placing it on the hearth. As she exits she meets the* CHILD FROM SYRIA *whose hand she clasps and leads over to the hay-filled shoe. The* CHILD FROM SYRIA *shakes her head and indicates a water jar she carries on her shoulder. Music off-stage, "We Three Kings of Orient Are," typifies slow-moving camels crossing the desert. The water jar is placed near the door for the camels as the* CHILD FROM SYRIA *stands on her threshold shading her eyes with her hands, watching for the shepherds and wise men. The* CHILD FROM HOLLAND *exits.*)

BROTHER AND SISTER: A little girl from Holland and one from the East! We learned about them in school. In Holland they leave hay on the hearth for Santa Claus' reindeer. In Syria they put sweet water on the doorstep for the camels of the three wise men.

(*Jump out of bed and watch, unseen, behind the* CHILD FROM SYRIA.)

(*The music changes to Handel's "Pastoral Symphony." Suddenly the* NIXIES *scamper in, crowding the* CHILD FROM SYRIA *away. They indicate to* SISTER *that they are hungry. She exits and returns with a bowl of porridge for each and finds that during her absence the* NIXIES *and* BROTHER *have banked the mantelpiece with evergreens. They eat hungrily and join hands with the children in a gay jig. As they dance,* SANTA CLAUS, *unseen by the children, again looks in the window.*)

SCENE III

Christmas Morning

(*Darkness slowly becomes light. The* CHILDREN *are asleep. Bulging stockings and* SANTA CLAUS *hanging the last gifts on the Christmas tree are seen.* BROTHER *and* SISTER *waken, hop out of bed, and embrace* SANTA CLAUS.)

BROTHER: Now, we've caught you!

SISTER: Never shall you get away.

SANTA CLAUS: Bless me! This is a surprise. I can't stay in such a small room as this. My home is the Earth.

BROTHER: Then call the whole Earth here to us.

SISTER: You are ours now.

SANTA CLAUS (*considers*): That might be a good plan. It would give me a chance to have a leisurely breakfast.

(*Goes to the door. Pan-pipes are heard mingled with sleigh bells. All* EARTH CHILDREN *and the* NIXIES *run in.*)

BROTHER AND SISTER (*surprised*): We have seen these children before.

SISTER: They came Christmas Eve to help make ready for you, Santa Claus.

SANTA CLAUS: These Earth Children kept Christmas before I did.

SISTER: Yes; we saw them giving gifts to the camels, the birds, and the reindeer.

BROTHER: And bringing us Christmas fire, and evergreens, and sweets.

SANTA CLAUS: Well, make haste, and strip the tree. I am about ready for a cup of coffee.

(*The* NIXIES, *with* SANTA CLAUS' *help, take gifts from the Christmas tree and lay them before* BROTHER *and* SISTER, *who nevertheless do not touch them.*)

SISTER (*offers the doll with dancing shoes to the* CHILD FROM NORWAY): Merry Christmas!

BROTHER (*gives his new skates to the* CHILD FROM ENGLAND): From Santa Claus!

BOTH CHILDREN (*distribute the gifts from the tree among the* EARTH CHILDREN, *keeping only their filled stockings*): Merry Christmas from Santa Claus!

(*All the Players dance about the Christmas tree singing, "There's a Wonderful Tree." The* EARTH CHILDREN *play their native folk games with* SISTER *and* BROTHER *and the* NIXIES.)

A Christmas Dream
By Mildred Abernethy Hayes

THE PLAYERS

MOTHER.
NATHALIE.
SAMMY.
BARBARA.
THE SANDMAN.
WINK.
BLINK.
RAGGED CHILDREN (any number).
TOYS:
    CANDLES.
    POP-CORN BALLS.
    BLOCKS.
    SOLDIERS.
    INDIANS.
    JACK-IN-THE-BOX.
    TOY ELEPHANT.
    TOY BEAR.
    TOY MONKEY.
    LADY RIDERS.
    COWBOYS.
RAG DOLLS.
CHARACTER DOLLS.
CLOWN DOLLS.
STORY BOOKS:
    OLD WOMAN IN THE SHOE.
    JACK HORNER.
    HANSEL AND GRETEL:
        THEIR MOTHER.
        THEIR FATHER.
        THE WITCH.
        THE DEW FAIRY.
        MANY GINGERBREAD CHILDREN.

A CHRISTMAS DREAM

By Mildred Abernethy Hayes

THE COSTUMES

Mother—Pretty house dress, as mature looking as possible if character is played by an older girl.

Barbara, Sammy and Nathalie—Night clothes in first scene.

Sandman—Close-fitting gray suit and gray cape. Carries a bag of sand over his shoulder.

Wink and Blink, Sandman's helpers—Smaller children dressed like him.

Ragged Children—Old tattered clothing.

Santa Claus—Usual costume.

Candle—Child is swathed in long sheet of stiff colored paper and wears pointed cap of yellow or orange paper. Any desired colors may be used and there may be two candles or a dozen.

Pop-Corn Balls—A cape covered with very full white crepe-paper ruffles is drawn in around the knees to a spherical shape. A little white cap may be added.

Blocks—Square hat boxes with holes cut for hands and head, and letters in color; or a block of large squares of heavy paper, laced together.

Soldiers—Uniforms may consist simply of hat, crossed strips of color across chest and wooden guns, or as elaborate as desired.

Indians—Indian suits may usually be borrowed.

Jack-in-the-Box—Clown suit may be worn; or merely ruff and pointed cap.

Elephant—Two children make one elephant. They wear loose-fitting gray sateen bags on their legs fastened well above the knee. The front child wears the head of gray sateen with paper-stiffened trunk. Both children bend over and a blanket of gray sateen is thrown over to give the effect of the elephant's body. A fancy blanket of bright colors may be placed over this.

Bear—Brown sateen sleepers with ears on the hood. Bear can wear roller skates if desired.

Monkey—Very small child in brown sateen sleepers, long

slender stuffed tail to match, bright monkey-jacket and little round hat.

Riders—Boys and girls in western cowboy dress.

Horses—Fasten two limber sticks about four feet long together at both ends. Slip over body of child rider. At one end fasten a horse's head and neck cut from light board, celotex or two pieces of heavy paper sewed together and slightly stuffed; place at end a flowing tail of tissue paper. A blanket of cambric or paper covers the space between, and the child's legs appear as the horse's. Hang artificial legs made from stuffed stockings on top of the blanket from the child's waist, giving the appearance of a rider on horseback. The "cowboys" wear fringed tissue paper chaps on the false legs.

The Old Woman in the Shoe—Long red skirt, black bodice and pointed hat to make her look tall. Her children wear attractive school clothes.

Jack Horner—Little jacket, flowing tie and long trousers.

Hansel and Gretel—Hansel, Gretel, Mother, Father, Witch and Dew Fairy wear costumes similar to those illustrated in "Free and Treadwell Second Reader."

The Gingerbread Children—Two large circles of brown cambric with faces drawn on with yellow crayon are stitched together and turned, allowing an opening large enough to slip over the child's shoulders.

Dolls—Rag dolls wear stocking masks and cotton dresses.

Character Dolls—Dresses as desired.

Clown Dolls—Clown suits.

STAGE DIRECTIONS

The stage is arranged with fireplace, big Christmas tree, rugs and reed chairs to look as much as possible like an American home on Christmas Eve. The curtain rises to show the mother, played by one of the teachers or an older girl, with three children grouped around her. She is reading the real Christmas story to the children from the Bible.

THE PLAY

SAMMY: Mother, will you please read "The Night before Christmas"? (*She reads, then lays down book.*)

MOTHER: Now, children, hang up your stockings while I turn down your beds. I shall expect you upstairs in just three minutes!   (*Children hang up stockings while she is gone.*)

NATHALIE: What do you hope Santa Claus will put in our stockings?

SAMMY: Candy, of course, and oranges and popcorn balls to make them nice and bumpy.

BARBARA: What I want most won't go in a stocking. I want a book.

NATHALIE: A book would, too, go in a *giant's* stocking!

BARBARA: Well, I don't want it in a giant's stocking. I want my presents in my stocking or on the Christmas tree.

SAMMY: I want a book, too.

BARBARA: You'd need an awfully easy book. There are so many words you don't know.

NATHALIE: Well, I want a doll, a character doll.

BARBARA: Oh, I want a doll, too, of course. We always get dolls for Christmas. Sammy's too big for a doll this year though.

SAMMY: I'd like a clown doll like the one we saw at the circus, and I want soldiers, and an Indian suit and blocks and, oh, anything Santa Claus has on hand.

BARBARA: I think you'll get one of those things. You know mother said Santa Claus had sent some things on ahead and not to look into cupboards and corners too much.

SAMMY and NATHALIE: Yes, yes!

BARBARA: Well, when I went for her handkerchief yesterday, a bundle stuck out from under her bed!

SAMMY and NATHALIE: Yes! Yes! Hurry! What was in it?

BARBARA: Well, I peeped just a little.

SAMMY: Oh, what was it?

NATHALIE: Tell us! Tell us!

BARBARA: Of course I won't tell a secret of Santa Claus' and Mother's! Of course not! But I think I know.   Don't you wish you knew, too?

NATHALIE (*turns to right of stage*): What's that? Oh, it's Christmas carols! (*The children listen. Carols are heard off-stage. One or several groups of children may participate here.*) We must go to bed now. Mother must be waiting. (*The children exit and* SANDMAN *enters, accompanied by* WINK *and* BLINK.)

SANDMAN: It's time Santa Claus was here. I hope he doesn't forget these children for they've been so good. Come Wink! Come Blink! Run to the windows and look out. Can you see Santa Claus?

WINK (*left*): No, there's no one in sight.

BLINK (*right*): I see someone in a sleigh. He's dressed in red and his sleigh is piled full. It must be Santa Claus!

SANDMAN: Yes, it must be Santa Claus!

BLINK: He's stopping here. He's coming in.
(SANTA CLAUS *enters.*)

SANTA: Hello, everyone! Are the children asleep? Show me their dreams, Master Sandman, for tonight I hope to make them all come true!

BLINK: I'm sure they want a pretty tree. Did you bring candles?

SANTA: Of course!

(*Produces them and* WINK *puts them on tree. At this point in the play the children's dreams of Christmas gifts they want begin to materialize. Each group, Christmas tree decorations, sweets, toys and story-book people appear on the stage in turn. If a curtain is not available between their entrances and exits, the stage may be darkened for a few minutes.*)

CANDLES (*enter and dance. Exit.*)

SANDMAN: The children are so fond of pop-corn. Let's have pop-corn balls on the tree.

POP-CORN BALLS (*enter and sing "The Pop-corn People," in "Songs of the Child's World," 1; Riley and Gaynor. Exit.*)

SANTA (*takes from his pack and hands real pop-corn balls to* WINK *and* BLINK *who put them on the tree. He then takes out, shows conspicuously and lays under the tree or gives to the fairies to place each gift as it is mentioned. The last article he takes out is a story book.*): Here's an easy story for Barbara. She can't read everything herself, in spite of teasing Sammy. But I think she can read "The Old Woman in the Shoe."

(*The curtain rises to show a large shoe of black oilcloth and red paper from which emerge the kindergarten children who dramatize this nursery rhyme with the help of an older girl who impersonates the "Mother."*)

WINK and BLINK (*curtain rises to show the blocks, impersonated by very tiny children*): Oh, see the blocks! Let's play with them. (*They arrange the children to spell several easy words, and at last Merry Christmas.*)

SANDMAN: All the children will like these blocks. And Sammy must have some soldiers. (*Enter* SOLDIERS.)

SANTA: And every real boy wants an Indian suit! (*Enter* INDIANS. *They sing any Indian song and dance.*)

SANDMAN: A story book for Sammy would surely finish his list.   Can you find one, Santa Claus?

JACK HORNER AND HIS PIE (*enters and repeats Jack Horner rhyme*).

WINK: Barbara loves jokes.   Don't I see a Jack-in-the-box in your bag, Santa Claus?   (*Jack-in-the-boxes bob up and down to music in large boxes.*)

SANDMAN: When the children went to the circus with their father last summer they had such fun. And ever since Nathalie saw that toy circus in a store window she has looked at it every day.

SANTA: Then she ought to have one—and here it is! (*Enter* CIRCUS ANIMALS. *They perform in character.*) I'll find a book for her.   Do you think she could read "Hansel and Gretel"?

WINK: Oh, I'm sure she could!   (SANTA CLAUS, SANDMAN *and his helpers leave stage during presentation of* "Hansel and Gretel" *as arranged in* "Free and Treadwell Reader," *Book 2.*)

SANDMAN (*returns*): It wouldn't be Christmas without dolls.   I have rag dolls, character dolls and clown dolls.   (*Enter dolls.   They dance.*)

SANTA (*returns and looks at the gift-laden tree*): I hope the children will like our presents.

SANDMAN: I know they will and we must hurry away before they find us here.

(*Exit* SANTA CLAUS, SANDMAN. *Enter the children, as on Christmas Day.   They investigate stockings.*)

SAMMY: Here's my clown doll!   My lovely soldiers!

BARBARA: Here's your Indian suit, too.   I knew that it was coming but I didn't tell you!

NATHALIE: My darling dolly!

BARBARA: My book. One for each of us! Why, what's the matter, Nathalie?

NATHALIE: I was thinking about our back-door neighbors. That little girl hasn't a single doll, and now I have four. I'm going to give her one of mine.

SAMMY: I want all of my presents myself. (*Thinks a minute.*) But I do like little lame Tommy. I guess I'll give him *one* of my Christmas gifts.

BARBARA: You know what our teacher said. When you give anybody something nice, you give to three people.

SAMMY: You don't mean that. How could you give one thing to three people?

BARBARA: Why, you give to the one who gets it, of course. And you give to yourself, because it makes you feel happy. And you give it to God.

SAMMY: Oh, let's divide our things with all the children in the block! (*Children run to back of stage and call.*)

ALL: Merry Christmas! Come and see our presents!

(*Enter group of ragged children. SAMMY, BARBARA and NATHALIE give each a gift. They all dance around the tree and sing "Around the Christmas Tree." Then, toys in arms, they face the audience and sing*):

Merry, merry Christmas unto you,
And a happy, happy New Year, too,
May the dear Lord bless you all the year through,
And we wish a Merry Christmas.

(*Or they may call out*)

Merry Christmas! Merry Christmas! We wish you a Merry Christmas and a Happy New Year!

The Christmas Party

By Carolyn Sherwin Bailey

THE PLAYERS

JOHN and BETTY—Americans.

TONY and CARMELLA—Italians.

PATSY and BRIDGET—Irish.

HANS and GRETCHEN—German.

PETER and JOAN—English.

IGOR and KATRINA—Russian.

CHERRY BLOSSOM—Japanese.

CARMENCITA—Spanish.

SANTA CLAUS—From the Salvation Army.

THE ELECTRICIAN—A boy or girl who can give an interpretive dance.

CHRISTMAS WAITS—Children who can sing.

THE COAL-AND-WOOD MAN—A boy large enough to carry a Yule log.

THE CHRISTMAS PARTY

By CAROLYN SHERWIN BAILEY

Two scenes. There is no change of setting. The time of the first scene is late afternoon of the day before Christmas. The second scene is lighted for Christmas Eve.

THE COSTUMES

All foreign children wear the costume of their native countries. The Italians have gay-colored handkerchiefs tied about their heads; Carmella has an embroidered apron and Tony a bright blouse. The Irish children wear green, rather shabby. Hans and Gretchen wear wooden shoes; Gretchen, a black velvet bodice, full skirt and white blouse; Hans, warm knitted cap and muffler, short jacket and velvet breeches. The English children wear blue sailor suits; Joan has long hair tied back from her face with a ribbon. The Russian children have very bright peasant costumes; Katrina's dress is embroidered in colors. Cherry Blossom wears a scarlet kimono and yellow obi, tied in a large bow. Carmencita has a white blouse, flowered skirt, embroidered apron, a black lace scarf and a tall comb in her hair. Santa Claus wears a bright red suit, trimmed with white, red cap, white cotton beard and mittens. He stands beside a kettle for money and has a bell. The Waits wear long scarlet capes and wreaths of holly. They carry paper scrolls with gilt lettering. The Electrician has two costumes. In the first scene he wears a workman's overalls and carries a coil of wire and tools. In the second scene he appears in a close-fitting suit of yellow to which are attached many floating streamers of yellow, orange and flame-colored gauze or dyed cheesecloth. He has a pointed cap that is shaped like a flame.

THE SETTING

The entire stage is covered with white cotton cloth, stretched tightly, to represent snow. A large back drop of paper or cloth is painted to look like the sky line of an American city, with tall apartment houses, factories, and smoke arising from these. Windows may be cut in the buildings, through which light shines when the daylight is gone. In front of this back drop are houses made of light screens in three sections, over the frames of which heavy paper is stretched, painted to show windows and doors. Such details as balconies, chimneys, and front stoops can be easily constructed of cardboard. Some of the windows are cut out, as well as the doors, to show action inside the house. In this case, a back wall must be constructed to conceal the back drop. These screen houses are set up at various angles at the back of the stage, with a little distance between, making narrow streets that are used for entrances and exits.

At one side of the stage Santa Claus and his kettle are seen. One or two houses may be arranged at sharp angles at the sides of the stage, so that there seems to be a Square upon which they face. At the side of the stage opposite Santa Claus there is a fir tree, wired for lighting. Drifts of snow may be represented with cotton batting piled on small boxes and dusted with frost powder. Lines drawn in charcoal on the stage will indicate the streets that give on the Square.

SCENE I

(SANTA CLAUS *rings his bell. He looks up and down the Square and shakes his head as if he were discouraged; looks in the kettle, swings his arms to keep warm. He rings his bell again.* JOHN *and* BETTY *enter from the opposite side of the stage. They investigate the tree.* THE ELECTRICIAN *enters and wires the tree with concealed bulbs. He exits.*)

BETTY: Well, we have a tree, anyway, but nothing planned for a party. I don't see much use in trying to have a community Christmas with so many strange children as have come to live in our town.

JOHN: Their fathers work here in the shops and factories. That is the reason they come. I just had a fight with young Tony, that Wop. Boy, that kid has fists!

BETTY: What did you fight about?

JOHN: Because I called him a Wop. That's what he is.

BETTY (*laughing*): You can't blame him, John. I know how you feel, though. I just hate to sit next to Bridget in school. I think they must cook onions every day in the year at her house.

JOHN: I told that thick-headed Hans what I thought of him, when he took the best bench in the manual-training room in school last week. If we are not careful these foreign kids will get the best of us in school.

BETTY: Carmencita wanted me to be her partner in the folk-dance class, but I wouldn't. I never play with the new girls.

(*She feels delightedly of the fir tree's branches; smells their fragrance. SANTA CLAUS rings his bell. She runs over and peers inside his kettle.*)

SANTA CLAUS: Not many pennies in there. Christmas isn't what it used to be. People are buying radios and automobiles and forgetting poor old Father Christmas. Here I have stood from morning until night for a week, ringing this bell, and nobody seems to know that I am alive.

BETTY (*opens her purse and drops some money in the kettle*): Poor old Santa Claus! It is hard for you. Perhaps you picked out a bad place to set up your kettle. These are the houses of the strangers along here, hardly an old resident among them. We children don't pay much attention to the stranger children. They don't know our games or talk as we do. The community Christmas tree has always stood here in the Square, but I am afraid that it will be very little fun this year.

SANTA CLAUS: Oh, I wouldn't go so far as to say that.

JOHN: Come along, Betty. Let's have a last look at the toyshops and then eat supper early. We might as well come back tonight and see the tree lighted.

*(They exit. SANTA CLAUS goes over to the tree and touches it as if he loved it. The stage is gradually dimmed as if the sun were setting. SANTA CLAUS rings his bell with a soft tinkling sound. Off-stage voices are heard, beginning the carol, "The first Noel, the angels did say." * The WAITS enter and, singing, stand in front of the houses. Lights may now be seen shining through the back drop and in the windows of the houses. PETER comes into the Square. His sister, JOAN, follows him.)*

PETER: Christmas Waits! See them, Joan, just like our Waits in England.

JOAN *(clapping her hands and dancing about)*: Oh, Peter, how friendly they are! I was feeling too lonesome to put up the Christmas greens, but here are our own carolers. I shall put a wreath on our door.   *(She exits and returns with a holly wreath that she and PETER fasten to the front of their house.)*

PETER: There's something else we need to make it a real English Christmas.   *(He whispers to JOAN.)*

JOAN: Yes, and —

(She whispers to PETER, pointing to SANTA CLAUS as if he were to be surprised. They exit. The caroling of the WAITS has roused the children in the houses. A door opens and BRIDGET, holding a candle high, looks out.)

BRIDGET *(speaking to PATSY, who joins her)*:   Whist, Patsy! The little people must have been here.   Look at the tree and the singers and the big green wreath next door. What would you say about it?

PATSY: Sure, I think it's the Christmas Child they're getting ready for in this city so far from our own green land. But Irish lads and lassies know how

---

*English, in "Fifty Christmas Carols of All Nations," Willis Music Co., Cincinnati, Ohio.

to welcome him best of all.   Go, Bridget, and set the table with a bowl of milk and bread for him, while I place the candle in the window to light his small feet.

(They go within the house, where BRIDGET *is seen laying the table with a white cloth and food while* PATSY *puts the lighted candle in the window. Lights are now seen farther down the Square.* HANS *and* GRETCHEN *appear carrying a well-filled bag between them.)*

HANS: They don't know how to trim a Christmas tree in this town.   All they can think of is to buy bulbs at the Electrician's store.   Here are apples that Grandmother sent us from the home orchard, and nuts I gilded.

GRETCHEN: And gingerbread horses and men that I baked myself.

BOTH: And the Christmas angel for the tip-top of the tree.

*(*HANS *and* GRETCHEN *set down their bag, empty it and begin trimming the tree.   They look to* SANTA CLAUS *for help in reaching the top branch but he nods and then goes to sleep over his kettle.* HANS *climbs up a snow bank and places the angel, made of paper, tinsel and gauze, on the top of the Christmas tree.   They then hang gilded nuts, apples and gingerbread toys from the branches. A sound at the other end of the Square surprises them and they watch silently as* CHERRY BLOSSOM *emerges from her house.   She places a bamboo table in front of the house upon which she lays some broken toys.)*

CHERRY BLOSSOM: There, now I shall make a Christmas wish for the souls of my dead toys and they shall all be made new.

(She bends over the toys, touching each one, as soft music, the "Pastoral Symphony" from Handel's "Messiah," is heard.   At the end of her silent prayer CHERRY BLOSSOM *hangs a string of lighted lanterns from poles so that they festoon her doorway.   Then she runs to the Christmas tree.)*

CHERRY BLOSSOM: How pretty! I never saw a tree like this before.

HANS: It is like those we have in Germany. What's that? Look at Igor and Katrina!

(The Russian children enter, their arms full of small branches of evergreen with which they make a path along the stage that leads to the tree. They lay the branches carefully side by side, tying some to make them more secure.)

CHERRY BLOSSOM: Why do you do that, Russian boy?

IGOR: We are laying a path for Saint Nicholas to walk along.

KATRINA: This is what we did in our country on Christmas Eve. Igor and I got these branches in the Park from the man who trims trees. We are trying to bring Saint Nicholas to this new land.

(As the path of evergreens is laid, the sound of a tambourine is heard. CARMENCITA comes, dancing, from her house, shaking a tambourine and carrying a great basket of fruit. She places the fruit beneath the tree.)

CARMENCITA: I can help with Christmas, too. This is the basket of goodies the Fairy Bufano leaves on Christmas Eve for children in Spain. But if you are a bad child, she will leave only a bundle of twigs.

(From the last house come TONY and CARMELLA. All the other children gather in wonder about the little creche they carry. On a tray of sand a cave is modeled of clay and covered with moss. Small twigs are placed in the sand for trees. Within the cave are seen the manger, the babe and toy animals.)

CARMELLA: Be very careful. Only look, do not touch.

TONY: We made it just like the Christmas mangers all children have in Italy.

(They place the creche near the Christmas tree. SANTA CLAUS *still dozes. The* WAITS *come forward to look at the creche and they sing, "God rest ye, merry gentlemen, let nothing you dismay."* The stage is darkened to indicate the end of Scene I.)*

SCENE II

(It is the dim light of early evening. SANTA CLAUS *is gone.* JOHN *and* BETTY *enter,* JOHN *holding a tool box in his arms,* BETTY *carrying a doll. They are so busy talking that they do not at first notice the change that has taken place in the Square.)*

JOHN: Well, as long as it's Christmas Eve I thought I might as well bury the hatchet and give Hans my tool chest. He does better woodwork in school than I anyway. He's making a desk set, all polished and everything.

BETTY: I have so many dolls that I thought—oh, look, John. Somebody has been here when we were gone. Look! See how the Square is ready for a Christmas party!

JOHN: Boy! So they have! So it is!

(He examines the colored lanterns and picks up some of CHERRY BLOSSOM'S *toys.* BETTY *dances about the tree, breaking off a bit of a gingerbread man and nibbling it.)*

BETTY: Gingerbread! *Mmmm.* Just like the cookies Gretchen brings for her lunch at school. Do you suppose, John, that Gretchen might have made these tree trimmings?

JOHN: It might be, with Hans' help, of course. Say, look at all the little Jap's old toys. *(He sets down his tool chest and takes out glue, hammer, string and nails. Begins mending the toys.)* I can put them together in no time, just as good as new.

BETTY: See the darling little barn with a manger and animals! Oh, see the basket of fruit! Carmen-

---

*"Fifty Christmas Carols of All Nations," The Willis Music Co., Cincinnati, Ohio.

cita must have left it here, for it is tied with the yellow ribbon she wore once to school.

(For a short time the children exclaim over the tree and finish mending CHERRY BLOSSOM's *toys.* BETTY *places her doll beside* CARMENCITA's *basket. Then they turn to the audience as if they had just discovered it.)*

BETTY: Look at all those people who have come to see our Christmas tree. It isn't lighted, John. What shall we do?

JOHN: I know that the Electrician wired it. I saw him. There are colored lights on wires all over it, red, blue, yellow, green. I will look for the switch.

(He goes behind the tree, but suddenly jumps back, looking startled. THE ELECTRICIAN *is with him.* THE ELECTRICIAN *is now dressed in yellow with flowing streamers of yellow, orange and flame color. He bows low to the children.)*

THE ELECTRICIAN: You sent for me?

BETTY *(timidly)*: Who are you?

THE ELECTRICIAN: I am the Christmas-tree Electrician.

JOHN: But you don't look like the man who wired our tree today. He wore overalls, and carried a lot of wire and tools.

THE ELECTRICIAN: The very same Electrician, at your service. I have been on a long journey since then.

JOHN: Where?

BETTY: Please do tell us about it.

(Losing their fear, the children come close to THE ELECTRICIAN, *touching his colored draperies and then drawing back as if they had been flames.)*

THE ELECTRICIAN: I went so far away that there were no cities. I traveled until I came to a green hillside in the shepherd's country where I saw a procession of kings and wise men, herders and little children all taking their way in the light of a star to the manger of Bethlehem. When they had passed, I grasped a ray of that Eastern star. I traveled on, carrying the ray of the Eastern star, until I came to another green country where the fairies and pixies were born. There, in a cottage beside a peat bog, I saw a candle burning in the window to light the footsteps of the Child born in the manger of Bethlehem. And I took one beam of the candle to keep the ray of the Eastern star burning. I traveled again until Ireland was far away and I came to a snowy street in the great city of London. Holly wreaths and mistletoe, puppet shows, spicy puddings in the bakeshops and singing children were making ready for Christmas. Down the London street came the Waits, singing carols. In every home the Yule log burned. I captured one spark from a Yule log to glow with the beam from the Christmas candle and the ray from the Eastern star. Then I hastened back to the city, for all the power of magic that electricity holds is not enough to light a Christmas tree. There must be starlight. There must be candlelight. There must be firelight.

JOHN and BETTY: Oh, light the tree, Electrician! Light the tree for us and all these people who are waiting to see it.

(THE ELECTRICIAN *dances, interpreting light. He circles slowly at first, raising arms and hands high above his head, the palms pointed like a candle flame. Then he dances faster until the streamers swirl as if aflame, gradually coming closer to the Christmas tree. As he reaches the tree, it bursts into light and he disappears. A slow waltz, gradually increasing in tempo, will suggest the free movement of such a dance.*)

(The WAITS *enter along the path of evergreens, singing:* "*This tree was grown on Christmas Day, Hail, Old Father Christmas.*"* *Following the* WAITS *is* SANTA CLAUS. *Behind him is* PETER, *helping* THE COAL-AND-WOOD-MAN, *who may be as sooty and grotesque as possible, to bring in a log.* JOAN *follows with a small puppet show.)*

SANTA CLAUS: Who said that we couldn't have a Christmas party? Why, I have found children from all over the world ready to share it with us.

PETER *(He helps* THE COAL-AND-WOOD-MAN *trim the Yule log with greens. The latter may give a character dance if he likes, or do some acrobatic stunts):* This isn't a very large Yule log, but we can have a jolly Christmas fire with it in the community house.

SANTA CLAUS *(leads* JOAN, *with her puppet theater, to the front of the stage.* CHERRY BLOSSOM *appears, clasps her mended toys joyfully, and she and* JOAN *set up the theater on the table):* Here, boys and girls, is a real Christmas pantomime.

JOAN: Would you like to watch my Punch and Judy show? I made it myself.

(Assisted by PETER, JOAN *shows her puppets.* PATSY *and* BRIDGET *come out of their house and watch.)*

SANTA CLAUS: Now for a Christmas jig.†   *(*PATSY *and* BRIDGET *dance.)*

SANTA CLAUS: I have some more Christmas dancers.

*(*CARMENCITA *enters, and, with* BETTY *for a partner, gives a Spanish folk dance with castanets.)*

SANTA CLAUS: Come, Igor and Katrina; dance for Saint Nicholas and the children.

(The Russian children, in high boots, enter along the path of evergreens, and dance.)

---

*"Songs in Season," A. Flanagan Company, Chicago, Ill.

†This national dance and the others that follow it may be found in almost any standard collection of folk dances.

SANTA CLAUS: Now, some dancers from an Italian fair.   (TONY *and* CARMELLA *enter and dance.*)

SANTA CLAUS: And now Hans and Gretchen, my German neighbors.   (HANS *and* GRETCHEN *enter and dance.*)

(*As the dancers finish, they group themselves about the Christmas tree, with the* WAITS *in the background. The children are all friendly. They examine the tree.* JOHN *gives* HANS *the tool box.* SANTA CLAUS *goes over to his kettle and peers inside. Astonished, he pulls out a Christmas cracker, which he tosses to* BETTY.)

SANTA CLAUS: A full Christmas kettle after all! Come along, boys and girls, and help me.

(*All the Players except the* WAITS *join* SANTA CLAUS *in tossing the Christmas crackers into the audience. When they have been distributed, and the caps put on, led by the* WAITS, *the Players step down from the stage and exit through the audience, singing a familiar carol in which the audience joins.*)

A Pageant of Time
By Anne Glenn Robeson

THE PLAYERS

LITTLE BOY—Dressed in school clothes.

LITTLE NEW YEAR—Wears a red toboggan suit, sweater, leggings and cap. The year, in numbers, is lettered across his jacket and bands of bells are on his wrists.

SPRING—In a green crepe-paper dress and band across forehead, lettered "Spring." She carries a large poster picture of spring.

SUMMER—In a yellow costume, similar to that of Spring and carrying a summer poster.

AUTUMN—In red dress and carrying an autumn picture.

WINTER—In costume like the others, but white. Carries a Christmas poster.

THE MONTHS—Twelve boys, wearing white blouses, dark trousers, peaked crepe-paper caps the colors of their seasons and each with a poster to represent his month.

THE DAYS OF THE WEEK—Monday, Tuesday, Wednesday, Thursday and Friday, are all little girls in dark dresses, white caps and aprons. Saturday is a boy in a play suit, carrying a football. Sunday is a boy or girl dressed for Sunday school.

THE SLEEP FAIRY—Wears a fairy costume or is dressed in a white sleeping suit.

A PAGEANT OF TIME

By Anne Glenn Robeson

On the day school started after the Christmas holidays we discussed the new year, using Emilie Poulsson's suggestions from "In the Child's World." "The Story of the Seasons" from the same book was told, and for several days the children reported on what the different months brought. These reports were printed and read by the children. A story, "The Twelve Months," in Elson's Second Reader, was told. This brought in the seasons. As we were to give a program at the Parent-Teachers' meeting the first Wednesday in February we talked about the possibility of a pageant and one little boy said, "Let's have the months come and help us!" So we decided that was exactly what we wanted to do. Then we reviewed the months and the seasons and what they give to us, and one child asked the question I had been waiting for: "Well, where does Tuesday come in?" So we talked about the days of the week, with their duties, and decided to add them to our pageant also.

One child brought a large picture entitled "Winter," that his mother had given him from an old magazine, and we decided to make posters of the months and the seasons to use in our pageant. Each picture was considered for suitability and whether it could be seen by the audience from the stage. After the children decided what gifts the seasons and the months brought, the teacher put their ideas into jingles. Posters were made to illustrate the jingle of each month. Children in the upper primary grades could make their own rhymes. The posters were on sheets of construction paper, 12″ by 18″, and could be clearly seen all over the assembly. The dialogue between "Little Boy" and the other characters was originated by the children.

The children discussed their costumes and the colors that should be used. They decided on these:

Green for spring leaves and grasses.
Yellow for summer sunshine.
Red for autumn leaves and apples.
White for winter snow.

The days of the week wanted to wear aprons and caps because they worked.

THE PAGEANT

(LITTLE BOY *is sleeping, at right front of stage, in a big arm-chair.* THE SLEEP FAIRY *enters and waves her wand over him and sings,* "The Land of Nod," *from Riley and Gaynor Song Book, No. 1. Then* THE SLEEP FAIRY *exits. Enter* LITTLE NEW YEAR.)

LITTLE NEW YEAR (*tugging at* LITTLE BOY): Wake up, Little Boy. Wake up and get busy.

BOY (*arousing dreamily*): What have I to do?

LITTLE NEW YEAR: Why, you must grow.

BOY (*gazing at* LITTLE NEW YEAR): Grow?

LITTLE NEW YEAR: Why, you must grow three ways; you must grow bigger, and you must grow wiser, and you must grow better.

BOY (*brighter*): Oh, yes, I see! If I keep my health rules I will grow bigger. (*Holds out both hands to show growth.*) If I study my lessons I will grow wiser. (*Puts finger on his forehead.*) And if I try to do right

I will grow better.   (*Hand over heart and pausing to think a second.*)   But you know it takes a long time to grow. Who will help me?

LITTLE NEW YEAR: I will be glad to help you.

BOY: And who are you?

LITTLE NEW YEAR (*bowing and pointing to himself*): Why, I am the Little New Year.   (*He comes to the front of the stage and sings, "Oh, I am the Little New Year, Oh, Ho," from "Songs and Games for Little Ones," Walker and Jenks. Then he turns to* LITTLE BOY *again.*)   I will help you, Little Boy.   I will call my children to help you too.   (LITTLE BOY *claps his hands and shows delight, and* LITTLE NEW YEAR *jingles his bells.*)   Come, my Seasons, come!

SPRING (*skips to front of stage, holding up her poster*):
   I am called the Merry Spring.
   Birds, leaves and flowers I bring.

SUMMER (*skips to* SPRING'S *side*):
   In summer time it's always gay,
   For children play outdoors all day.

AUTUMN (*skips to front of stage*):
   I paint the golden autumn leaves,
   And stack the grain in harvest sheaves.

WINTER (*joins her sisters*):
   Sparkling fires! Skating's zest!
   Boys and girls like winter best!

(*They all sing "Song of the Seasons,"* Kindergarten Story-Hour Song Book.)

LITTLE BOY: But a season is a long time to grow in.

SEASONS: We each have three months and they can help you, we know.

(THE SEASONS *step back of* BOY *and stand in a row, while* LITTLE NEW YEAR *rings his bells.*

LITTLE NEW YEAR: Come, my Months.

(THE MONTHS *enter, one at a time, and each stands in the center-front of the stage to give his lines, then steps back, opposite* THE SEASONS, *where they form a semi-circle.*)

JANUARY:
>January brings cold and snow,
>Warmly wrapped to school we go.

FEBRUARY:
>Hatchets, cherries, cupids, too.
>February brings to you.

MARCH:
>March comes blowing low and high.
>See our kites tug as they fly.

APRIL:
>April brings the Easter bunny,
>Hides his eggs in meadows sunny.

MAY:
>Round the Maypole dance and sing.
>Try and spy a fairy's ring.

JUNE:
>June brings roses, red and sweet.
>Barefoot boys go down the street.

JULY:
>Gather seashells in July.
>Watch the sailboats drifting by.

AUGUST:
>August brings us cantaloupe,
>And lots of other fruit, we hope.

SEPTEMBER:
>Goldenrod now lights the lane,
>And children start to school again.

OCTOBER:

> October brings us Hallowe'en,
> When ghosts and witches may be seen.

NOVEMBER:

> Thanksgiving Day and darker skies.
> Turkey, nuts and pumpkin pies!

DECEMBER:

> Christmas trees I bring, and holly,
> Not another month so jolly!

LITTLE BOY (*speaking to* THE MONTHS): Now I know you all, and each one of you is mine, but even a month is a long time to grow in. Haven't you any shorter time?

MONTHS: We each have four weeks and each week has seven days. Little New Year, can't you call the Days?

LITTLE NEW YEAR (*rings his bells and calls* THE DAYS, *one at a time.* MONDAY *comes to front of stage with a small washtub and doll's dress*):

MONDAY:

> All your washing I will do.
> School begins on Monday, too.
> (*Pantomimes washing.*)

TUESDAY (*enters with toy ironing board and iron and doll's clothes*):

> Clothes I'll iron smooth and neat,
> We must keep clean from head to feet.
> (*Pantomimes ironing.*)

WEDNESDAY (*enters with sewing bag, spectacles and a stocking on a darning egg*):

> I'll mend your suits and darn your hose.
> You must look tidy in your clothes.
> (WEDNESDAY *pantomimes mending.*)

THURSDAY (*enters with broom*):
> I'll sweep your house with all my might.
> I'll dust it well and clean it right.
> (*She sweeps.*)

FRIDAY (*she has a pan and spoon*):
> My bread I'm sure will win the prize.
> I'll stir your cakes and bake your pies.
> (*She stirs with a spoon and mixing bowl.*)

SATURDAY (*enters in play suit*):
> Here I am, your Saturday!
> Come out doors with me and play.
> (*Holds a ball toward* LITTLE BOY.)

SUNDAY:
> Come with me to Sunday school,
> And learn about the Golden Rule.

(DAYS OF THE WEEK *go to back of stage and fill in the space left between* THE MONTHS *and* SEASONS.)

LITTLE BOY (*to* LITTLE NEW YEAR): Well, Little New Year, you have many workers.

LITTLE NEW YEAR: Yes, and if you will use them they will help you, too.

LITTLE BOY (*earnestly*): I will use them every day and I'll grow so big, and so wise, and so good that I guess in a year you won't know me.

LITTLE NEW YEAR: Well, after next Christmas, I'll come to see you again, but you won't know me either, for I'll be an old, old man!

ALL: Oh, yes, we will know you, for then you will be called "Old Father Time."

(*As a finale to the pageant six little girls dressed in crepe-paper costumes, each of a rainbow color, skip in, one at a time, throw a kiss, and form a line across the front of the stage. They sing:*

FIRST CHILD:
Here's a kiss for Monday,

SECOND CHILD:
And one for Tuesday, too.

THIRD CHILD:
Here's a kiss for Wednesday,
And I think most of you.

FOURTH CHILD:
Here's a kiss for Thursday.

FIFTH CHILD:
And Friday on your cheek.

SIXTH CHILD:
A kiss for Saturday makes it,—

ALL:
A kiss for each day in the week!

(This should be repeated with backs turned to the audience, throwing the kisses over their shoulders. The words may be sung by all the characters as the curtain goes down.)

The Rabbit Who Wanted Red Wings
By Carolyn Sherwin Bailey

THE PLAYERS

THE LITTLE RABBIT.

MOTHER RABBIT.

MR. BUSHY TAIL—A Gray Squirrel.

MR. PORCUPINE—A Prickly Animal.

MISS PUDDLE DUCK—Who Likes the Rain.

MR. GROUND HOG—Old and Wise.

THE RED BIRD.

AS many other forest creatures as possible—Rabbits, Squirrels, Young Ground Hogs and Birds.

THE RABBIT WHO WANTED RED WINGS

By Carolyn Sherwin Bailey

Scene   I—*In the Rabbits' House*
Scene   II—*In the Forest*
Scene III—*The Same as Scene II*

STAGE DIRECTIONS

A curtain of brown and green cambric is cut in an uneven pattern of holes and fringed. This is hung at the front of the stage so that it extends one-quarter to one-third of the distance down, not hiding the players, but giving the effect of dappled shadows in the woods. If stage lighting is possible, lights thrown behind this fringed curtain will make it look as if sunlight were shining through. These lights are switched off to indicate night.

A plain rug of moss green or brown covers the floor of the stage. This is suitable for both scenes.

Scene I has a back drop of heavy muslin painted to look like the bark of a tree. There is a rabbit hole in it large enough for the animals and birds to enter and exit. This makes the children of the audience feel themselves inside a tree. Back of the hole are seen green bushes and flowers, which may be planted in pots. Small plain chairs, a low table, a bed and a stove, both of which may be constructed of packing boxes, furnish the rabbits' house. Bunches of carrots and parsley, baskets of beans, lettuce heads and anything else rabbits enjoy are seen all about and give color to the stage setting. Vegetables are piled on the table.

Scene II has a back drop upon which are painted the trunks of tall trees. Strips of brown cambric cut irregularly and having bark and leaves painted in large patterns are stretched from the floor of the stage to the ceiling for forest trees. Trees in tubs may be used instead if desired. Paper flowers grow from the ground. At one side is the Wishing Pond, a little round pool made of silver paper or tinfoil with shrubs and flowers built up to make a low bank around it. A low stepladder behind the trees makes it possible for the Players to enter as if from the branches. Mr. Ground Hog's home is on one side of the stage, a hole cut in the back drop with many twigs, brush and nuts scattered in front of it. Mr. Bushy Tail's house is behind one of the trees. Miss Puddle Duck lives near the Wishing Pond.

THE COSTUMES

Canton flannel suits cut in one piece to cover the hands and feet are the foundation for all the costumes. These are made with close-fitting caps to which ears may be sewed. The Little Rabbit is white and he wears a short jacket. There are slits in the back of the jacket through which his folded red wings appear surprisingly. The wings are made of plaited crepe paper and are fastened by a string around his neck so that he can pull them out of sight when the play requires this action.

Mrs. Rabbit wears a large checked gingham apron and a folded white kerchief. The ears of both the rabbits are very long and lined with pink cambric, and their tails are tufts of lamb's wool or cotton batting.

Mr. Bushy Tail's costume is gray with tiny pointed ears. His large waving tail is made of raveled roving which may be lightly wired so as to stand up over his back.

Mr. Porcupine's suit is of some mottled pepper-and-salt fabric. His quills are made of narrow strips of brown paper twisted into lamp-lighter shape. These are spotted with white ink and sewed thickly to the back of the costume so they stand out straight. His ears and tail are small.

Miss Puddle Duck's costume is of greenish yellow with feathers and wings made of crepe-paper feathers sewed to the foundation. She wears red rubber boots or overshoes, a bonnet and a small colored shawl folded over her shoulders. She carries a green umbrella under one wing.

Mr. Ground Hog is padded out underneath his grayish brown costume so as to be very roly-poly. He has large claws drawn with charcoal on his hands and feet. A mask with tiny eyes and a black pointed nose would make him realistic and he carries an ear of corn which he gnaws from time to time. The Red Bird wears scarlet, her feathers being vivid in color.

The Forest Creatures wear bird costumes made of bright paper feathers fastened to their costumes, or they are dressed as squirrels, ground hogs, and porcupines.

SCENE I

Afternoon in the Rabbits' House

(Mrs. Rabbit *is seen bending over the stove making a carrot stew. The* Little Rabbit *is playing. He hops about the stage in time to music, but tires of this. Then he teases his mother for one of the carrots. Next he plays ball in time to waltz music with one of the lettuce heads, but gives up when his ball rolls into a corner. He peers out of the rabbit hole, up and down the forest, and then returns to* Mrs. Rabbit, *pulling her apron.*)

The Little Rabbit: I want something new to play. I want some carrot stew now. Tell me a story. Tell me what to do next, Mammy.

Mrs. Rabbit (*shakes her head until her ears flop in impatience, wipes her paws on her apron and turns, brandishing her spoon at* Little Rabbit): Once upon a time there was a little White Rabbit with two beautiful long pink ears and two bright red eyes and four soft little feet—such a pretty little rabbit, but he wasn't happy.

(*A sound of chattering and scampering is heard outside, and in through the rabbit hole comes* Mr. Bushy Tail *carrying a bag of corn over his back. He pours out half of the corn on the table.*)

Mr. Bushy Tail: Good evening, Mrs. White Rabbit. Here is some fine corn I gathered on my way home and thought you would like for your supper.

(*Seats himself in one of the chairs with his tail draped over the back.*)

Mrs. Rabbit: Thank you, Mr. Bushy Tail. Corn mush is so good for my Little Rabbit. Would you like a bowl of my fresh carrot stew?

Mr. Bushy Tail: No, thank you, Mrs. Rabbit. I like to sharpen my teeth on a hard nut at this hour of the day.

(*Tries to rise, and discovers that the* Little Rabbit *has hold of his tail.*)

MRS. RABBIT: Naughty Little Rabbit! Let go of Mr. Bushy Tail.

THE LITTLE RABBIT: Oh, Mammy, I wish I had a long gray tail like Mr. Bushy Tail's.

(MR. BUSHY TAIL *exits through the rabbit hole, waving a good-bye. Just as he goes, in comes* MR. PORCUPINE, *looking very important and fierce. He stalks about the stage bristling with quills.*)

MR. PORCUPINE: Good evening, Mrs. Rabbit. I thought I would stop in on my way home to see if you were safe. Towser was out today and I had to keep a close watch on him, for he looked as if he smelled rabbits. I just sent him home howling.

MRS. RABBIT (*holds* MR. PORCUPINE'S *paw in hers, shaking it warmly*): Thank you, Mr. Porcupine. What would we rabbits do without you. Will you stay to supper?

(*Suddenly hops up in the air, for* LITTLE RABBIT *has pulled out one of* MR. PORCUPINE'S *quills and is trying to see if it is sharp by sticking it in his mother.*)

THE LITTLE RABBIT: Oh, Mammy, I wish I had a back full of quills like Mr. Porcupine!

MR. PORCUPINE (*pats* LITTLE RABBIT'S *head*): Your mother doesn't. No, thank you, Mrs. Rabbit, I cannot stay to supper. I must be getting on. A safe night to you.   (*Exits.*)

(*Quacking is heard off-stage.* MISS PUDDLE DUCK *enters, waddling, and looking backward into the forest.*)

MISS PUDDLE DUCK: Good evening, Mrs. Rabbit. It looks like rain. I thought you would like to know. I don't care. I have my little red rubbers on.

(MISS PUDDLE DUCK *opens her umbrella and waddles about the stage in time to music.* LITTLE RABBIT *follows her, imitating her waddling and looking down at her rubbers.*)

MRS. RABBIT (*looks out of the hole*): The sun is still shining. You like the rain so much, Miss Puddle Duck, that you feel it on a fair day. May we give you some corn? It was a gift from Mr. Bushy Tail.
(*Fills* MISS PUDDLE DUCK's *basket.*)

THE LITTLE RABBIT: Oh, Mammy, I wish I had a pair of red rubbers like Miss Puddle Duck's!
(MISS PUDDLE DUCK *exits, quacking her thanks loudly.*)

MRS. RABBIT (*fills a bowl with carrot stew and sets it on the table for* LITTLE RABBIT. *She looks at him sorrowfully*): Once upon a time there was a little White Rabbit, and he went on wishing and wishing and wishing until his Mammy was clean tired out with him. She was so tired out that she made up her mind to go for a walk and leave him to eat his supper alone.
(*Puts on a bonnet and exits through the hole.*)

THE LITTLE RABBIT (*between mouthfuls*): I wish I had a long gray tail. I wish I had a back full of quills. I wish I had a pair of little red rubbers.
(*He suddenly sees old* MR. GROUND HOG, *who has entered and seated himself by the stove.*)

MR. GROUND HOG: Always wishing, wishing for something you haven't got! (*Looks all about to see that no one is listening. Then whispers to* LITTLE RABBIT) Why don't you go down to Wishing Pond out in the forest? If you go to Wishing Pond and look at yourself in the water and turn around three times in a circle, your wish will come true. A little bird told me.
(LITTLE RABBIT *is amazed. He leaves his supper and peers out through the rabbit hole. Suddenly he scampers off. Old* MR. GROUND HOG *fills the bowl full of carrot stew and seats himself at* LITTLE RABBIT's *place at the table.* MRS. RABBIT *returns and finds* LITTLE RABBIT *gone.*)

MRS. RABBIT: Where is my baby?
(*Old* MR. GROUND HOG *continues his supper and says nothing.*)

SCENE II

In the Forest

(*The* LITTLE RABBIT *finds himself alone in the forest. He wanders about peering behind trees, picking flowers and dropping them, and hopping about in time to music until he discovers the Wishing Pond. He bends down to look in it. The* RED BIRD *hops twittering down from a tree and stands on one side of the pond to take a drink.* LITTLE RABBIT *looks admiringly at the* RED BIRD.)

THE LITTLE RABBIT (*as if he were speaking to himself*): Look at yourself in the water. Turn around three times in a circle. Your wish will come true. I wish I had a pair of nice little red wings. (*Looks at his reflection in the Wishing Pond. Turns around three times as the* RED BIRD *watches.*) My shoulders feel queer, as if something prickly were growing under my jacket.

(*Rubs his shoulders.*)

THE RED BIRD: Let me help. Wings do hurt when they first start sprouting.

(*She helps pull the red wings through the* LITTLE RABBIT'S *jacket. Then she flies about the stage twittering in joy.*)

THE LITTLE RABBIT (*joyfully*): My wish has come true. I have a pair of red wings.

(*He looks at them in the Wishing Pond. He flaps them by pulling the string underneath his jacket. Then he and the* RED BIRD *hop and dance together about the forest. They are interrupted by a stamping of feet off-stage.* MRS. RABBIT *is calling him. She enters, looking anxiously behind the trees.*)

MRS. RABBIT: Oh, where is my dear little son? His supper is waiting for him. His bed is ready. How can I close the rabbit hole for the night with my Little Rabbit away?

THE LITTLE RABBIT: Here I am, Mammy.

(*Goes to her side, but* MRS. RABBIT *does not recognize him.*)

MRS. RABBIT: Have you seen a little white rabbit

with two beautiful long pink ears and two bright red eyes and four soft little feet—such a pretty little white rabbit even if he does ask for things he can't have?

THE LITTLE RABBIT: Here I am, Mammy. See my new red wings!

MRS. RABBIT: I don't know you. No rabbit ever had wings. Oh, what shall I do if my little son is lost?

(Goes about the forest stamping her feet and looking in all the nooks. Exits, wiping her eyes. The RED BIRD *goes back to her tree. The stage is dim, for night is coming on.* LITTLE RABBIT *tries to fly up to the* RED BIRD'S *nest but is unable. He goes to a tree in front of which is a large pile of nuts and raps on the bark.)*

THE LITTLE RABBIT: Mr. Bushy Tail! Kind Mr. Bushy Tail, please may I sleep in your house all night?

MR. BUSHY TAIL *(comes out from behind his tree)*: Who is it?

THE LITTLE RABBIT: The little rabbit who wanted red wings.

MR. BUSHY TAIL: I never saw a rabbit with red wings. There must be some mistake.

(Goes back of the tree again. MR. PORCUPINE *is seen near a tree.)*

THE LITTLE RABBIT: Mr. Porcupine! Kind Mr. Porcupine, may I sleep with you tonight?

MR. PORCUPINE: Who are you?

THE LITTLE RABBIT: The little rabbit who wanted red wings.

MR. PORCUPINE: I am sorry to say I don't know you, and my quills would tear your wings so it doesn't seem sensible to take you in for the night.

THE LITTLE RABBIT (*sees* MISS PUDDLE DUCK *on her nest at one side of the Wishing Pond*): Miss Puddle Duck! Kind Miss Puddle Duck, may I sleep in your nest all night?

MISS PUDDLE DUCK (*waddles over and around the* LITTLE RABBIT): Who is it?

THE LITTLE RABBIT: The little rabbit who wanted red wings.

MISS PUDDLE DUCK: I never saw a rabbit with red wings. I must be dreaming. (*Returns to her nest, spreads her wings and goes to sleep.*)

MR. GROUND HOG (*pokes his head out of his hole. Sees* LITTLE RABBIT *and chuckles*): Ha, ha; so your wish came true!

THE LITTLE RABBIT: Mr. Ground Hog! Kind Mr. Ground Hog, may I sleep in your house all night?

MR. GROUND HOG (*emerges and leads* LITTLE RABBIT *to the hole*): I can't say how comfortable you will be. I use beech nuts and branches for my bed, but if you can stand it you are welcome.

(LITTLE RABBIT *tries to settle himself for the night in* MR. GROUND HOG'S *hole. The stage is darker, and good-night twitterings of birds are heard.*)

THE LITTLE RABBIT: Mammy! Mammy! Mammy!

(*Off-stage* MRS. RABBIT *may be heard softly stamping. A host of little forest creatures, squirrels, porcupines and ground hogs come in carrying flashlights. They dance about and peer in at* LITTLE RABBIT, *now asleep, but tossing about restlessly. They chatter and laugh at his wings. Then they exit and the stage is entirely dark for a few moments to indicate the passing of the night. Lullaby music from victrola or piano will be effective.*)

SCENE III
Morning in the Forest

(*The birds, one at a time, awake twittering. Then their songs are heard from bird whistles. Light comes, dimly and then brighter, to simulate bright sunshine. Many birds flock from among the trees, some jumping down from the low branches. LITTLE RABBIT gets up from his bed stiffly, and comes out to the center of the stage. His wings are draggled. The birds fly about him in surprise.*)

THE RED BIRD: Here is that funny little rabbit who wanted red wings.

A BLUEBIRD: Can you sing?

A WILD CANARY: You have no bill!

A ROBIN: What kind of worms do you like best?

THE RED BIRD: Will you not fly for us?

THE LITTLE RABBIT (*decides to try his wings. He goes behind a tree and climbs the low stepladder. He seems to be standing on a limb. He spreads his wings and jumps down, but falls in the bushes outside MR. GROUND HOG's door. He is unable to get up*): Mammy! Come and help me! Mammy! Oh, Mammy!

MR. GROUND HOG (*stretches himself and emerges from his hole*): What is the matter? Don't you like your red wings?

THE LITTLE RABBIT: No! No!

MR. GROUND HOG (*helps him out of the bushes*): Why do you not go to the Wishing Pond and wish them off again?

(*The LITTLE RABBIT, followed by the twittering birds, goes to the Wishing Pond. He looks at himself in the water, turns around three times and pulls his wings inside his jacket out of sight by means of the string. The RED BIRD touches the LITTLE RABBIT's jacket where the wings were. All the Forest Creatures crowd around very much surprised. MRS. RABBIT enters unobserved. She seems to have been out all night.*)

MRS. RABBIT (*approaches the Forest Creatures anxiously*): Have any of you good folk seen a little white rabbit with two beautiful long pink ears and two bright red eyes and four soft little feet—such a pretty little rabbit? (*Stamps to call him.*)

LITTLE RABBIT (*pushes through the Forest Creatures to his mother*): Here I am, Mammy! Oh, here I am!

(*They clasp paws and dance while the birds and animals, joined by* MR. BUSHY TAIL, MR. PORCUPINE, MISS PUDDLE DUCK *and* MR. GROUND HOG, *circle about them.*)

(*The circle then breaks, the birds either sing or fly in time to interpretative music, and the animals dance.*)

MUSIC FOR THE PLAY

Clapping, Slow Time, for Rabbits' Stamping
"A Potpourri of Rhythm".................*Mabel S. Rogers*

Rolling Balls, for Little Rabbit's Ball Play
"Rhythms for the Home, Kindergarten and Primary".........
Francis M. Arnold

"Old Dan Tucker," for Mr. Ground Hog
"Folk Dances from Old Homelands........*Elizabeth Burchenal*

Ducks
"Rhythms and Dances for Elementary Schools"..............
Dorothy La Salle

Rabbit in the Hollow
"Rhythms and Dances for Elementary Schools"..............
Dorothy La Salle

Flying Birds
"Rhythms for the Home, Kindergarten and Primary".........
Francis M. Arnold

The Bunny
"Small Songs for Small Singer"............*W. H. Neidlinger*

Mr. Squirrel
"Small Songs for Small Singers,".............*W. H. Neidlinger*

Little Birdie
"Small Songs for Small Singers".............*W. H. Neidlinger*

The Little Ducks
"Dramatic Games and Dances for Little Children" ....
Caroline Crawford

The Little Rabbits
"Dramatic Games and Dances for Little Children" ....
Caroline Crawford

"Frisk, Little Squirrel"
"Songs of the Child World, Number 3".......*Riley and Gaynor*

"Mr. Bunny Rabbit"
"Songs of the Child World, Number 3".......*Riley and Gaynor*

"In the Forest".............................*Carl Reinecke*

Nocturne from "Midsummer Night's Dream".....*Mendelssohn*

All on the King's Highway
By Mary E. Carpenter

THE PLAYERS

THE LITTLE OLD WOMAN.

THE LITTLE OLD WOMAN'S CAT—A very small child in cat mask and furry suit.

THE SHEPHERDESS.

THE OLD GARDENER.

THE PRINCE.

ATTENDANTS TO THE PRINCE—As many as you wish.

AN OLD FARMER WOMAN—Slightly deaf.

VILLAGERS—As many or as few as you wish. Villagers are not necessary.

ALL ON THE KING'S HIGHWAY

By Mary E. Carpenter

THE SCENERY

The scenes take place in front of a cottage past which the King's Highway runs. Hang your stage with a background of draperies. Place screens at stage, right, for front view of a cottage. Place an old bench in front of the screens. A wooden peg is in the wall near the door. The cottage would be very gay if the panels of the screens could be covered with large sheets of beaver-board or heavy paper painted over with a wash of sunny yellow paint. A door and windows with shutters could be painted over the yellow wash in a contrasting color such as brown or dark green-blue. Enclose the small dooryard with a low green hedge made with boxes covered over with dull green flannel, or a "brushwood fence" made by placing dry tree branches together in a rude fashion. Outside the hedge or fence is the highway on which are two large rocks, one at extreme left and one center back. Make the rocks by covering over large portable steps, boxes and tables with gray flannel. Any addition of potted plants skillfully placed to give illusion of plants growing from behind the rocks will add charm.

THE COSTUMES

Well-illustrated editions of the famous old English fairy tales will answer every problem of dress for every character. Also many of the modern primers and lower-grade readers in which the text of old fairy tales is illustrated will be of help.

PROPERTIES

Jug of cream.
Basket of butter pats.
Bag of fleece.

Baskets of lilies.
Cuckoo clock.
Baskets of eggs.

STORY OF THE PLAY

Once there was a Little Old Woman who found she had plenty of cream and butter but no eggs for Easter. She tried to think of a way whereby she could get them. The town was so far off she couldn't walk there and be back in time to milk her cow. At last she thought she would see if she could turn her butter into eggs, so she sat out on the King's Highway where many strangers passed. Each stranger was in need of the things the Little Old Woman possessed, so she kindly gave them that which they needed and in turn the strangers gave the Little Old Woman what little they had in thanks for her kindness. Just as the Little Old Woman was giving up hope of ever having any eggs for Easter, an old farmer woman saved the situation.

THE PLAY

(*A* LITTLE OLD WOMAN *comes from her fields to the front of her cottage carrying a jug of cream and a basket of butter pats. She sits down on an old bench and places the jug and basket beside her. The* OLD WOMAN'S KITTEN *has followed at her heels and now curls up beside her and watches every move she makes. The* LITTLE OLD WOMAN *lifts up the jug again and as she looks contentedly at the cream in it she speaks to her* KITTEN.)

LITTLE OLD WOMAN: My, my, kitty, this is thick rich cream my good cow Bessie gives me every morning and every night! I am sure there's not another person in the whole countryside blessed with so good a cow and such sweet milk!

(*The* KITTEN *answers the* LITTLE OLD WOMAN *in an agreeing tone.*)

KITTEN: *Meow!*

(*The* LITTLE OLD WOMAN *then looks into her basket and again speaks to her* KITTEN.)

LITTLE OLD WOMAN: And my, my, kitty, what fresh golden butter pats I have made from Bessie's cream! Surely there's not another person in all the countryside blessed with so good a cow and such butter pats!

(*The* KITTEN *answers again in an agreeing tone.*)

KITTEN: *Meow! Meow!*

(*The* LITTLE OLD LADY *removes her shawl and hangs it on the peg by the door.* KITTEN *runs in front of her.*)

LITTLE OLD WOMAN: My, my, kitty, come out from under my feet or I will surely step on you and hurt your tail. (*When she has hung her shawl on the peg she goes back to the bench and takes up the basket of butter pats. She then empties the basket, placing the pats beside her.* KITTEN *tries to get up on the bench to see what the* LITTLE OLD WOMAN *is doing but she scolds him.*) Down, kitty, down! You'll not have your saucer of fresh milk if you get your paws into my butter pats. Now mind!

(*The* KITTEN *answers as though he were pouting.*)

KITTEN: *Meow!*

LITTLE OLD WOMAN: Why, kitty!

(*The* KITTEN *sulks on the opposite end of the bench while the* LITTLE OLD WOMAN *carefully counts her butter pats and puts them back into the basket, one by one.*)

LITTLE OLD WOMAN (*counting her butter pats*): One . . . two . . . three! What a good cow Bessie is! Four . . . five . . . six! I wonder if other people have such fine butter pats? Seven . . . eight . . . nine! And every one weighing a good ounce over a half pound! Ten . . . eleven . . . twelve! And one extra for good luck just fills my basket. But what good luck have I with Easter coming and not an egg to be had? And what's Easter without colored eggs on the table? Bessie is a good cow and I can turn her cream into butter, but no matter how hard I may try, I can't turn butter into eggs!

(*The* KITTEN *has been listening to the* LITTLE OLD WOMAN *and surprises her by answering her in a sad tone, as if to say,* "No.")

KITTEN: *Me-e-ow!* (*And shakes his head sadly,* "No.")

LITTLE OLD WOMAN: If I could go into town

I could sell my butter pats and buy some eggs for Easter, but it is so very far I couldn't walk there with my poor feet and get back in time to milk Bessie.

KITTEN: *Me-e-ow!*   (*As if saying "No."*)

(LITTLE OLD WOMAN *stoops down and gets an empty saucer from under the bench. As she pours fresh milk from her jug she calls to her* KITTEN.)

LITTLE OLD WOMAN: Here, puss, puss, puss. . . . kitty, kitty, kitty. (*She pets the* KITTEN *gently.*) Nice puss?

(*The* KITTEN *answers as if saying "Yes."*)

KITTEN: *Meow! Meow!*

LITTLE OLD WOMAN: Here is lovely fresh milk for you.   You may drink it while I am gone.

(*The* KITTEN *looks up wonderingly at the* LITTLE OLD WOMAN *and asks her, mewing, where she is going.*)

LITTLE OLD WOMAN: I'm going to see if I can turn my butter pats into eggs.   I will be back by sundown but, mind, you run into the house and keep the mice from my pantry or there will be no more of Bessie's milk for you!   (*The* KITTEN *obeys the* LITTLE OLD WOMAN *and runs to the cottage door. As he is just about to disappear behind the door the* LITTLE OLD WOMAN *calls after the* KITTEN.) Let the flies buzz on the windowpanes but don't let the mice play in the pantry!

(*The* KITTEN *turns around and pokes his head out of the door to answer.*)

KITTEN: *Me-e-ow!*

(*The* LITTLE OLD WOMAN *gets her shawl, takes her basket of butter pats and starts off singing a merry little tune as she goes. She turns back once more to find* KITTY *watching her and calls back to him.*)

LITTLE OLD WOMAN: There may be luck in the extra butter pat, kitty!

(*The* KITTY *nods his head to agree that there might be luck.*)

(*The curtains close for a few minutes and reopen to show the* LITTLE OLD WOMAN *hobbling over to a big stone which is on the edge of the King's Highway. She looks up and down the road and then sees a bird flying above her head. She speaks to the bird.*)

LITTLE OLD WOMAN: How pretty you are, little bird, flying in the bright sunlight. People are not like you this morning; they do not seem to be out in the sun as you are. I had better place my basket behind this rock, in the shade where the sun can't get at the butter and spoil my fresh pats. (*The* LITTLE OLD WOMAN *looks at her foot and then takes off her shoe.*) There must be a stone in my shoe! (*The* LITTLE OLD WOMAN *is surprised not to see a stone fall out of her shoe. She then notices her heavy stocking is wrinkled. As she straightens her stocking and starts to put her shoe on again, she notices a shadow coming near her, and, on looking up, finds it is a sweet little* SHEPHERDESS *who is weary and stops for a moment as the* LITTLE OLD WOMAN *speaks to her.*)

LITTLE OLD WOMAN: Have you come from a long distance, little Shepherdess?

SHEPHERDESS: Yes, I have come from very far. Do you see the blue hills that rise behind the bend in the road? There my sheep are grazing, and I must be back to herd them before sundown.

LITTLE OLD WOMAN: Where are you going, and why must you go, little Shepherdess?

SHEPHERDESS: I am going to town with this small bag of fleece which was washed and dried on the grass. I must sell it and with the coins I get for the fleece buy fresh butter pats for my mother who is making Easter cakes and needs fresh butter.

LITTLE OLD WOMAN: Now that is very lucky!

SHEPHERDESS: Very lucky?

LITTLE OLD WOMAN: Yes, for there is no need of your going further when I have the very fresh butter pats which will surely make your mother happy. There is no one in all the countryside who has a better cow than my Bess, or better butter pats than I myself make from her milk. And as for me and what I wish, I may as well have your small bag of fleece as this basket of butter pats!

(LITTLE OLD WOMAN *gives her basket to the* SHEPHERDESS, *and the* SHEPHERDESS *gives the* LITTLE OLD WOMAN *her bag of fleece.*)

SHEPHERDESS: I am very lucky not to have to travel any further to the town; now I will surely be back in time to tend my sheep. This basket full of the best butter pats in the whole country-side will make wonderful rich Easter cakes.

(*The* SHEPHERDESS *skips merrily down the road in the direction from which she came. The* LITTLE OLD WOMAN *watches her out of sight and then turns to look at the big bag of fleece.*)

LITTLE OLD WOMAN: My, my, I may as well have a bag of fleece as a basket of butter pats, for neither the fleece or butter will ever be a basket of eggs, and the little shepherdess needed the butter very much. I have all the milk and butter I wish every day from good Bessie.

(*As the* LITTLE OLD WOMAN *looks into the bag of fleece again, she speaks to herself.*)

It is clean white fleece, fluffy and soft, with all the greasy oil of the sheep washed out of it. But how I wish this bag was filled with eggs.

(*As the* LITTLE OLD WOMAN *is still looking at her fleece an* OLD GARDENER *comes from the opposite direction from which the*

SHEHPERDESS *went. He is carrying a basket of Easter lilies, and mumbles to' himself as he walks along. He does not see the* LITTLE OLD WOMAN *but she hears what the* GARDENER *is complaining about as he passes.*)

GARDENER: Easter! Easter is almost here and no one will buy my lilies. Lilies are growing everywhere in the country this year so I must take mine to the city where people have no gardens.

(*The* LITTLE OLD WOMAN *speaks to the* GARDENER *and startles him.*)

LITTLE OLD WOMAN: You are very tired; sit down here on this rock a while. You have a long way to travel if you are going into town. It will do you good to rest here a while.

GARDENER: No, I' can't stop. I must sell my flowers.

LITTLE OLD WOMAN: Your lilies are very beautiful. Did you raise them in your own garden?

GARDENER: Yes, they come from my garden, but their beauty will be of no use to me unless I sell them, for my little girl is ill. My little girl is always cold . . . cold even now that spring has come, and the warm sun. My wife tells me I must bring back some warm lamb's wool.

LITTLE OLD WOMAN: Lamb's wool? Then you have no sheep on your farm?

GARDENER: No, I have very few animals; only flowers. I have almost every kind of flower in my garden. But I must be on my way to town or I will never be back with the wool.

(*The* GARDENER *starts to go, but before he is out of sight the* LITTLE OLD WOMAN *runs after him and calls out.*)

LITTLE OLD WOMAN: Don't be in such a hurry!

GARDENER: If I stay here, wasting my time talking to you, it will be sundown before I am halfway into town.

LITTLE OLD WOMAN: Wouldn't a bag of newly washed fleece please your wife?

GARDENER: That's what I'm going to town for, and I will be lucky if I am able to get newly washed fleece.

LITTLE OLD WOMAN: Then you are very lucky for, see, this bag is full of fluffy, newly washed fleece which was dried on the grass only this morning. It is yours in exchange for your lilies. I may as well have your lilies as this bag of fleece, for I have so many blankets and quilts in my attic there is no room for more.

GARDENER: Oh, my! Thanks, thanks! I will take this bag of wool home to my wife. Her clever fingers know just how to pull the fleece apart and spread it out to fill the little patchwork quilt she has made. As soon as it is done our little girl can sit in the sunshine and wrap her new downy spread about her. She will be warm and comfortable.

LITTLE OLD WOMAN: Well, I certainly hope so. The winds are a bit sharp these early spring days; bad for children unless they are well wrapped up.

GARDENER: Well, a happy Easter to you, kind old woman, and if you ever come our way just stop in at the house by the mill. We'll be glad to give you anything you may choose from our garden. Good-day and a happy Easter!

(*The* LITTLE OLD WOMAN *watches the* GARDENER *out of sight and then goes slowly back to the stone where she was sitting as he passed.*)

LITTLE OLD WOMAN: Yes, a happy Easter, and lilies just as white as eggs, but no eggs! Yet I may as well have this basket of lilies as a bag of fleece, I'm sure.

(*The* LITTLE OLD WOMAN *places the basket of lilies beside her, and yawns, for she is becoming drowsy.*)

LITTLE OLD WOMAN: This sun is very warm. (*She takes off the shawl.*). It seems to make me drowsy.

(*Any number of villagers may pass by just before the* PRINCE *enters. If desired they may take part in an English folk dance.* LITTLE OLD WOMAN *dozes. Soon a young* PRINCE, *attended by a large bodyguard, comes down the road. Just as they come near the* LITTLE OLD WOMAN, *one of the* GUARDS *speaks to the* PRINCE.)

FIRST GUARD: This is more than half the way to the castle where the princess is waiting for you, your Royal Highness!

PRINCE: That may be, but I have decided not to go another step until one of you dullards helps me out. Here I am going to see the fair princess to present her with a cuckoo clock. Now how can I give her a cuckoo clock and at the same time tell her I love her? There is no romance in a cuckoo clock, I tell you. I shall go no further! (*The* PRINCE *turns and sees the* LITTLE OLD WOMAN *sleeping. He also sees her flowers.*) Why, I would rather take those lilies to the princess than this clock. It would be easier to give her flowers and say, "I love you," than to tell her so with this clock!

SECOND GUARD: The Little Old Woman is sleeping!

PRINCE: Splendid! Now it will be simple to exchange this clock for her flowers. The Old Woman hasn't sold a lily today, and if she had she would not be able to buy such a clock as this with her few coins.

THIRD GUARD: The bargain is more than fair, your Royal Highness.

FOURTH GUARD: You had better hurry, your Highness, before she hears us and spoils our plans.

(*The* FOURTH GUARD, *who is quite fat, takes the clock from the* PRINCE, *tiptoes over to the* LITTLE OLD WOMAN *and exchanges the clock for the lilies. He makes such a clownish sight of himself as he tries to be quiet that the other* GUARDS *and* PRINCE *laugh at him when he isn't looking. When he gives the flowers to the* PRINCE *the latter speaks to him.*)

PRINCE: I will make you a knight of the secret service for this brave deed you have done. Never have I seen anyone show such bravery!

(*The other* GUARDS *laugh among themselves, knowing the* PRINCE *is joking, but the* FOURTH GUARD *becomes very vain and struts off leading the procession down the road toward the castle. The* FIRST GUARD *speaks as they go.*)

FIRST GUARD: I hope the cuckoo doesn't strike the hour before we are out of sight, for then we would surely be caught!

(*The* GUARDS *and the* PRINCE *disappear. Soon the* LITTLE OLD WOMAN *awakens as if from a dream. She looks about her as though expecting to see some one and is surprised to find herself alone. She then looks at her basket and speaks as she sees the clock.*)

LITTLE OLD WOMAN: They were here! It was not a dream after all. Here is the very cuckoo clock and my lilies gone! I wonder if it truly was the prince? Well, it doesn't really matter who it was, for if they are happy with the lilies I am sure I may as well have this clock as the flowers. Neither the lilies nor the cuckoo clock could ever be a basket of eggs. How I have wasted my day sitting here trying to turn my butter pats into eggs! (*The* LITTLE OLD WOMAN *then thinks to herself of the exchanges she has made since she first came to the highway.*) Butter pats to a bag of fleece, a bag of fleece to a basket of lilies, and now a basket of lilies to a cuckoo clock . . . but no eggs for Easter! I may as well go home to kitty and Bess.

(*The* LITTLE OLD WOMAN *picks up her shawl and puts it around her, and takes the cuckoo clock and starts down the road toward home. She is startled suddenly by the sound of someone yawning very loudly, and turns to see a pair of stretching arms appear above the rock on the opposite side of the road. The* LITTLE OLD WOMAN *stands gazing and wondering who it can be. Soon an* OLD FARMER WOMAN *picks herself up from behind the rock, still stretching and yawning. She then begins to mumble to herself.*)

FARMER WOMAN: Oh, the day's wasted!

LITTLE OLD WOMAN: You are right, the day is wasted!

(*The* FARMER WOMAN *is surprised when she sees the* LITTLE OLD WOMAN *watching her. She speaks to the* LITTLE OLD WOMAN, *and holds one hand to an ear, for she is deaf and wishes to hear every word.*)

FARMER WOMAN: Hey? What's that you say?

LITTLE OLD WOMAN: I say, the day is wasted.

FARMER WOMAN: What's wasted?

LITTLE OLD WOMAN: The day!

FARMER WOMAN: Oh, the day. It's wasted! Mm, I guess that's so, and I don't want to go home for there's not so much as a cat's "meow" or a dog's bark to greet me when I open the door of my hut. Not so much as a dog's bark!

THE LITTLE OLD WOMAN: Here, what would be better for you to have than a cuckoo clock?

FARMER WOMAN: That's a fine clock you have.

LITTLE OLD WOMAN: It is yours to keep the loneliness away every hour of the day and night. It will keep you company and sing to you every hour.

FARMER WOMAN: My clock?   No, that's not my clock!

LITTLE OLD WOMAN: This clock will do you more good than it will me, so you may as well take it and hurry along home!

FARMER WOMAN: But I can't repay you for such a clock.   I have no gold to my name.   (*The* LITTLE OLD WOMAN *gives the clock to the* FARMER WOMAN.   *The* FARMER WOMAN *then quickly runs behind the rock and brings out a basket which she offers to the* LITTLE OLD WOMAN.   Here, this is all I have in the world . . . just a basket of eggs!

LITTLE OLD WOMAN: Eggs! Eggs! Why they're better than gold!

FARMER WOMAN: Gold?   Well, they're yours with many thanks, and now I must hurry home and put this clock on the shelf above my fireplace.

(*The* FARMER WOMAN *starts to go off.   She mumbles to herself as she goes.*)

She says that eggs are better than gold?   Well, I don't know.   Anyway I'd rather have my cuckoo clock.

(*The* LITTLE OLD WOMAN *watches the* FARMER WOMAN *out of sight and then opens her basket of eggs and looks at them as she speaks to herself.*)

LITTLE OLD WOMAN: Yes, eggs are better than gold or butter pats or a bag of fleece or Easter lilies when you haven't any and Easter is coming.

(*The* LITTLE OLD WOMAN *starts down the road happily humming.   She then speaks wonderingly to herself.*)

I wonder if kitty and Bessie will understand when I tell them I did turn my butter pats into eggs after all.

(*She chuckles and goes on down the road.*)

Mothering Day
By Helen M. Reynolds

THE PLAYERS

Mother.
Father.
Little Jane—The Youngest.
Margaret—About Twelve Years Old.
Tom—About Fifteen Years Old.
Susan—Ten Years Old.

MOTHERING DAY

By HELEN M. REYNOLDS

(MOTHER *sits in a low chair, her favorite magazine in her lap. At the left of the stage, near the center, is a high-backed chair. A small table near this holds a book or two. A workbasket stands on the other side. At the right of the stage, facing it from the audience, a door opens into the dining-room; at the left, one leads to the street.*)

MOTHER: What a quiet, restful hour with my magazine! My family really does understand how to keep Mother's Day! With the lovely spring-time calling me into my garden and all the spring sewing calling from my workbasket the hours go very quickly and my magazine was still unopened. I think Father must have helped plan this. The children insisted that they were going to wash the dishes after dinner and set the table all in readiness for our Sunday-night supper. How quiet they are! I've not heard even the rattle of the silver for a long time. They seem to be longer than usual in their "clearing away." Father and Jane should be back soon, too, from their visit to Grandmother. She will be glad that she had her visit on Mother's Day too! This having a day all our own is a pleasant thing for mothers. I wonder just how it began?

(*Steps are heard in the hall.* FATHER *and* JANE *enter.*)

FATHER: Heigh-ho! Here we are again, Mother.

JANE: Yes, and Grandmother was so pleased to see us, and she liked the little pink geranium so well. She said she was glad it was Mother's Day, so that we were sure to come to see her. She laughed when she said that. It really was a joke, wasn't it,

Mother, for Father and I always go to see her every Sunday afternoon. She told me to tell you she was coming to spend the day with you on Wednesday if that is convenient. Is it convenient, Mother?

MOTHER: Yes, Jane, very convenient.

JANE: Then I must be sure to get home early on Wednesday to see her.

FATHER: Where is all the rest of the family?

MOTHER: I was just wondering that myself. Those dishes must have been washed long ago and the table set for supper too! Some plans must be under way! Jane, I believe you look a bit guilty.

(JANE *looks at* FATHER *and smiles, trying to look quite uncon-scious.* FATHER *looks expectantly toward the dining-room door. From the dining-room suddenly come sounds of smothered laughter and cries of "sh, sh." A resounding rap is heard on the door of the dining-room.* JANE *runs to open the door, while* MOTHER *in surprise rises from her chair.* FATHER *seems to be in the secret and stands beside* MOTHER *to view the procession which enters. First comes* SUSAN *carrying, draped over both hands, a beautiful scarf. Behind her comes* TOM *bearing a footstool. Next follows little* JANE *who has slipped into the line, with a pot of daffodils she has found ready for her just inside the dining-room door, followed by* MARGARET *bearing a cake. When the door is opened by* JANE *there is a hearty shout from)*

TOM: A celebration for Mother's Day!

FATHER: Hear, hear! We all do celebrate Mother's Day!

SUSAN: Come, Mother dear, you must sit upon this throne.

(*While she speaks she gives to* FATHER *the gay scarf with which he covers the high-backed chair.* SUSAN *leads* MOTHER *to the chair.*)

MOTHER (*smiling upon the group and speaking with great ceremony*): My dear family, is it not enough that you

relieve me of all work after our feasting and grant to
me a long quiet hour for my reading?   But I welcome
you all in this celebration.   What is now to befall me?

SUSAN: Oh, Mother dear, there are many things
about Mother's Day that we think you have never
dreamed of!   Father, you tell her the strange story
that you read in the huge "Book of Days."

FATHER: You think, dear madam, that the celebration of your special day is a modern matter,
but long ago in the days of great-great-grandmother
in old England, in early springtime, there was set
aside a Sunday for "Mothering Day."   On that Sunday, the little maid who had gone from her home in
the village to work in the great house on the hill,
the boy from the cottage apprenticed to the silver-
smith in the town, the school boy from the great
house off at boarding school—all came home to see
their parents, especially to see the mother.   Each
one brought with him a trinket, a little gift, for his
mother.   So your children today have brought their
"trinkets."   Mine is the scarf which Susan has spread
upon the throne of the mother of this house.

MOTHER: I wondered only today while I sat here
so quietly resting by myself just when the thought
of this day arose.   I had no notion that dear great-
great-grandmother, whose picture hangs upon our
walls, once celebrated, too, her "Mothering Day."   I
am grateful, John, for the beautiful scarf that deco-
rates my throne.

TOM: I'm sure, Mother, that you are not quite
comfortable upon your lofty throne until I kneel and
place beneath your feet the footstool which I have
made myself.   It is of strong fir wood from the forests

made with copper nails hand-hammered, with a silk covering well-padded as a rest for your tired feet.

MOTHER: Thank you, my son, it will be pleasant to think of your labors when I stop to rest and find this footstool ready for my use.

JANE: My "trinket," Mother, is a growing one— daffodils just unfolding. Long weeks ago Margaret helped me plant the little dry brown bulbs. We left them a long time as the bulbs began to grow and the green stalks and buds appeared. I'm glad now I did not neglect them.

MOTHER: Place them here upon the table, Jane. We shall all enjoy them. I am glad they are just opening. For many days they will give us pleasure. We'll all remember the care you and Margaret gave them.

SUSAN: My "trinket," Mother, is just something made with my hands, a tiny little holder of linen worked with your initials and padded softly, to save your hands when you pour the tea and the teapot is very hot. I have written on this little old-time scroll a poem which I found. It made me think of you. It is written by Anna Hempstead Branch. I would like to say it for you.

MOTHER: I shall be glad to listen, my child.

SUSAN (*recites poem very thoughtfully and with appreciation, looking at her mother*):

HER HANDS

"My mother's hands are cool and fair,
  They can do anything.
Delicate mercies hide them there
  Like flowers in the spring.

When I was small and could not sleep,
  She used to come to me,
And with my cheek upon her hand
  How sure my rest would be.

For everything she ever touched
  Of beautiful or fine,
Their memories living in her hands
  Would warm that sleep of mine.

Her hands remember how they played
  One time in meadow streams,
And all the flickering song and shade
  Of water took my dreams."
                    —*Anna Hempstead Branch.*

MOTHER: Those are very lovely thoughts, Susan.
Ever since your father gave me my little red "Book
of Modern Verse" I have known and reread many
times those "Songs to My Mother." They are my
"lessons." Do you know why I say that, children?

(*Children do not answer. They look a bit puzzled, smile at
each other and at* FATHER.)

MARGARET: I think we do, Mother. Father did
not tell you all the tales he found in the great "Book
of Days," all the stories of long-ago Mothering Day.
Upon the table stands a Simnel cake which I have
made for you, and I will relate its story. Long
years ago in old England in the days when people
had no surnames, only first names, in a little country
place there lived a good man Simon and his wife,
Nelly. They were left alone in their cottage. Their
children were married and living in cottages of their
own but all were coming to visit on "Mothering
Day." The two old people wished to prepare a
feast worthy of their coming but they had little to

do with and were quite troubled to know what they could prepare.

Simon said, "There's still a little fine flour made from our good wheat, ground for us by the good miller."

"Yes," said Nelly, "and there is still some of the dried fruit saved from our Christmas pudding. We have eggs, too, from our own hens. Yes, I think we can have a real feast," said Nelly.

So she broke the eggs into her largest bowl, stirred in the treasured fine, white flour and the fruit saved from the plum pudding.

"Now it's well stirred and all ready to be boiled," said Nelly.

"Boiled," said Simon. "What an idea. It should be baked."

"No, indeed," said Nelly. "It must be boiled."

Sad to say the two old people could not agree. Simon knew it must be baked and Nelly was sure that baking would ruin it. They quarreled long and loudly, forgetting all about the coming of their children and the expected feast. All at once the good wife laughed.

"How foolish we are," Nelly said. "Here we are quarreling and the pudding is not yet ready for tomorrow. Why can we not boil it first and bake it afterwards. Then it will be sure to be well-done."

"Well said," laughed old Simon. "Good wife, you are right."

In the quarreling some eggs had been broken and after the pudding had been boiled Nelly spread the egg all over the outside before she baked the good pudding before the fire. When it was finished it was like a crisp cake, soft inside, with the fruit giving it a rich flavor. The story of the quarrel and its happy ending was told in many a cottage, and for years the cake prepared for Mothering Day was known as a Simon-Nelly cake. Gradually the story was forgotten and the people, in their hurry, called the cake for Mother's Day a Simnel cake.

Herrick gives us these words which the maiden repeats as she presents her companion with a Simnel cake to give to his mother on his visit to her:

"I'll to thee a Simnel bring
'Gainst thou goes a-mothering;
So that when she blesses thee,
Half that blessing thou'lt give me."

—Suggested by data in "Chambers Book of Days," Vol. I, page 335.

MOTHER: Indeed, Father's big "Book of Days" did yield new tales of this happy day. I wonder if any other mother has had such lovely thought given to celebrate this Mothering Day.

FATHER: And now for the Simnel cake! Lead the way, Susan.

(FATHER *takes* MOTHER'S *arm within his own.* JANE *is on the other side and they all leave through the door into the dining-room,* MARGARET *carefully bearing the cake. They all sing "Home, Sweet Home" on their way to the dining-room. In the distance the song is heard and finally dies away. Someone behind the scenes turns off the stage lights.*)

The Maypole
By Carolyn Sherwin Bailey

THE PLAYERS

A BOY OF TODAY.
A GIRL OF TODAY.
A TRUMPETER.
THE STRAW MAN.
THE LEAF BOY.
JUNIPER BERRY.
CORN MOTHER.
MAY ROSE.
FAUNS—As many as there are Dryads.
DRYADS—As many as there are Fauns.
PEASANT CHILDREN—Enough to play some merry folk
    games.

THE MAYPOLE

By CAROLYN SHERWIN BAILEY

THE SCENERY

If possible have the play out of doors. At one side, right, is the front of a cottage. For an indoor stage, paint this cottage on beaver-board, white and green, with a door that will open, and flowers in the window boxes. Outdoors, a child's playhouse can be used. In the center of the stage is a green and high hedge which conceals a Maypole. Make this hedge of paper leaves fastened thickly to a light screen that stands on rollers, or weave a lattice of twigs or reed in which leafy boughs can be twined. This screening should be as compact as possible and completely hide the Maypole. At the left there is a dense green woods. Indoors, make this forest of green gauze curtains fringed and slit to blow about, or sew brown cambric shapes of tree trunks and green leaves to the curtains. Outdoors, arrange for real trees. A rustic seat is beside the cottage door.

THE COSTUMES

The Boy and Girl of Today wear everyday clothes. The Trumpeter wears a purple velvet jerkin, doublet and yellow silk hose. He carries a gay tin trumpet. The Straw Man is grotesquely dressed like a vagabond with straw sewed to his shabby clothes, his shoes and even his cap. Juniper Berry wears full green skirts covered with gray-green leaves, a blue bodice and a wreath of blueberries about her hair. She carries a little broom made of twigs. The Leaf Boy's suit is close-fitting and entirely covered with leaves cut in the shape of those of the oak. They cover his hands and his sandals. He, too, wears a wreath of leaves. Corn Mother has a green tunic made long, with full yellow trousers showing underneath. She may have a girdle with hanging ears of corn. May Rose has a fairy-like dress of pink tulle. The Fauns are in one-piece, close-fitting brown suits; cardboard horns are arranged on elastic to wear on their heads. The Dryads have short white cheesecloth tunics, wreaths of flowers and garlands fastened to their robes. They are barefooted or in sandals. The Peasant

Children are in folk costume of England, Germany, Sweden and France, the countries that had the earliest Mayings.

THE STORY OF THE PLAY

A Boy of Today starts out a short time before sunrise on May Day to hang a May basket upon the door of a girl who is his friend. After he reaches the cottage where she lives and sounds her knocker a surprising thing happens. The May basket is discovered to be filled, as were the May baskets of villagers of long ago, with eggs, candles, butter, cheese and loaves. As the sun rises a trumpeter sounds a call that takes these children back through the ages to the times when the forests were the home of fauns, and trees were inhabited by dryads. Characters of long ago Mayings enter and show the children of today the customs which have led up to our festival of dancing about the Maypole.

THE PLAY

(*It is hardly light. Bird whistles sounding one at a time off-stage indicate the dawn. The* TRUMPETER *peeps out of the woods and then goes back. The* BOY *appears from behind the hedge, goes on tiptoe to the cottage and hangs the May basket on the latch. The* GIRL *peeps out of a window, unseen by the Boy and then softly closes it.*)

THE BOY (*lifts the corner of the cloth that covers the basket*: I think Betty will like her May basket. I gathered some violets for it. There is a bunch of them for her to wear to school today. I put in some marigold seedlings she can set out in her garden. They are wrapped up in moss. Mother made a little frosted cake, and there are two lollipops. . . .

THE GIRL (*runs out through the door and holds her May basket close*): Lollipops! Oh, you are good, Bobby. May I guess the flavor? Vanilla.

THE BOY: No, not vanilla for May Day.

THE GIRL: Lemon?

THE BOY: No, not lemon. Can't you think of the lollipop colors that belong in a May basket?

THE GIRL (*looks puzzled and repeats aside the rainbow colors*): Red, orange, yellow, green, blue, purple. . . . Red, for apple blossoms. Green, for green leaves. Yes, I think you put a red, rose-flavored lollipop and a green lime-flavored one in my May basket.

(*Lifts up the covering and peeps in the basket. Looks amazed as she takes out a tiny jar of clotted cream.*)

THE BOY (*also amazed*): What's that, cream? I didn't put any cream in. Let me look. *Takes out an old-fashioned tallow candle and a white egg.*) Well, I don't understand this!

THE GIRL (*empties the basket*): A pat of butter and a little loaf of bread! Just like housekeeping, Bobby. I love your May basket for me; but you said lollipops, bad boy. (*Shakes her finger at him.*)

THE BOY: I tell you I did buy you two lollipops, Betty. I never put those queer things in. . . . What's that? (*The trumpet is heard.*)

TRUMPETER (*enters at left, running, and blows his trumpet toward the audience. The* BOY *and* GIRL *seat themselves, amazed, beside the cottage door, where they seem to be invisible to the other Players but may themselves watch the action*):
"We've been rambling all night,
    And sometime this day:
And now returning back again,
    We bring a garland gay.

"A garland gay we bring you here;
    And at your door we stand;

It is a sprout well budded out,
The work of our Lord's hand."
—Old English Maying Rhyme.

(FAUNS *and* DRYADS *enter, the* FAUNS *from the stage left, the* DRYADS *at stage right. Each carries a flowering branch. They twine these over the cottage door, at the windows, and lay them at the doorstep. Then they dance around the hedge and at the front of the stage. Interpretive music for dancing fauns and dryads may be the fairy theme from Gilbert and Sullivan's "Iolanthe," "Midsummer Night's Dream" by Mendelssohn, or MacDowell's "To a Wild Rose." At the finish of the dance the* FAUNS *and* DRYADS *find hiding places for themselves in the woods from which they leap out from time to time.)*

THE TRUMPETER:
"Behold the ancient customs
By which the folk made gay
Within the pleasant greenwood
Upon the first of May."
—May Day Festival Book.

THE STRAW MAN (*enters from behind the hedge in a very dignified way. Swaggers about a bit. Goes up to the bough-trimmed cottage and pinches off a flower or two upon which he treads*): Sometimes I wear a cloak of snow and a crown of ice. Sometimes I am dressed in brown moss. But wherever I go it is winter on earth. I don't believe in keeping May Day. I have come to put a stop to it. Hanging May baskets is a silly custom. I don't believe in hanging May baskets. Hullo, here are some flowers trying to blossom. This cannot be allowed.

(*Looks down and tramps about the stage as if stepping on the wild flowers, but does not see the* LEAF BOY *who peers around the hedge at him.)*

LEAF BOY (*comes bravely up to the* STRAW MAN, *although he is smaller*): Here, you mustn't do that. You mustn't step on my flowers. Go away from here. Go back to the cave in the mountain where you belong.

STRAW MAN: Who are you, little Leaf Boy, that you think you can tell me what to do? Look how much bigger than you I am. Try to drive me away if you can.

(*Advances, shaking his fists at the* LEAF BOY.)

LEAF BOY: Smaller or bigger, I have come to bring the May and you have got to leave.

(*This is the cue for the* LEAF BOY *and the* STRAW MAN *to wrestle as hard as they can. This should be a good fight. The* STRAW MAN *is clumsy and is presently worsted by the* LEAF BOY. *The* TRUMPETER *watches and blows a note of triumph as the* STRAW MAN *falls to the ground, draggled and silent. The* FAUNS *and* DRYADS *come out and carry the limp, conquered* STRAW MAN *off the stage.*)

THE TRUMPETER:

"Now carry we Winter out of the village,
The new Summer into the village.
Welcome, dear Summer,
Green little Corn."

—Very old Ode to the May.

JUNIPER BERRY (*appears in the doorway of the cottage sweeping the threshold neatly and with energy. She pretends to brush down cobwebs and even sweeps underneath the seat without seeing the* BOY *and* GIRL): We have been housecleaning for the three last days of April, I and my sister, Rue, who is so tired that she will not be able to keep May Day. For years we two sisters, Juniper Berry and Rue, have been taking our way through cottage and castle, village and town, cleaning, polishing, and making all things fragrant for the first day of May.

(*Sees the* LEAF BOY, *lays down her broom and crosses to him. He stretches out his arms to catch her, but she eludes him coquettishly. They chase each other about the hedge in time to running music. At last he catches her and they dance together. Either the "Hansel and Gretel" dance in "Rhythms and Dances," by La Salle, or the well-known "Klappdans" may be used. At the end of the dance the* LEAF BOY *and* JUNIPER BERRY *curl up on the ground at either side of the hedge.*)

CORN MOTHER (*runs in with a gliding rhythm from behind the hedge, and looks inquiringly at the ground and sky*):

> "Send thou us a still small rain,
> That the fields may fruitful be
> And vines in blossom we may see;
> That the grain be full and sound,
> And wealthy grow the folks around."
>
> —Old Greek Chant to the Corn.

(*The* CORN MOTHER *glides up and down imaginary furrows scattering seed. Such music as Chopin's "Raindrop Prelude," the "Chanson Triste" by Tschaikowsky, or "The Death of Ase" by Grieg, will inspire the sweeping rhythm needed for this interpretive dance. Presently the mischievous* FAUNS *and the graceful* DRYADS, *one by one, slip from the forest and follow the* CORN WOMAN *in her planting.*)

FAUNS AND DRYADS:

> "In the merry, merry springtime,
> When the apple blossoms blow,
> Oh, that's the time for planting seeds,
> For that's the time they grow, they grow.
>
> "So here's one for the blackbird,
> And one for the crow,
> One for the cutworm,
> And three for to grow,
>
> And three, and three for to grow."
>
> —Old Corn Planting Song.

(*One by one the* FAUNS *and* DRYADS *go back to their trees and the* CORN WOMAN *is left alone. She discovers a flower upon the ground that the* STRAW MAN *tried to kill. She kneels beside it covering it tenderly with her hands. Then she rises and stretches her hands to the sky.*)

CORN MOTHER:

> "Dear May, we bid you welcome,
> Green Grass, we bid you welcome."

(*While the* CORN MOTHER *is speaking* MAY ROSE *appears where the growing blossom was. Corn Mother turns and sees her. The* FAUNS *and* DRYADS *run out and circle curiously about her.*)

FAUNS AND DRYADS (*as they dance in a circle about* MAY ROSE):

"Little May Rose, turn round three times,
    Let us look at you round and round!
    Rose of the May, come to the greenwood away,
    We will be merry all.
    So we go from the May to the roses."

—Old French Maying Rhyme.

(*The circle opens, and* MAY ROSE *dances alone. Tschaikowsky's "Sleeping Beauty" waltz or one of the Strauss waltzes may be the music she interprets. The* FAUNS *and* DRYADS *may form the chorus in this dance. If desired the singing game, "The Sleeping Beauty" in "Dramatic Games and Dances," by Crawford, may be used as the motif for May Rose, the* LEAF BOY *playing the prince and* JUNIPER BERRY *the fairy. At the end of this music the* CORN MOTHER *comes to the front of the stage.*)

CORN MOTHER:

"The King and Queen of May
    Are coming this way
    And all their company.
    Throw flowers in the street
    Beneath the dancing feet
    Of all the company.
    They bring the lovely tree
    With ribbons fair to see.
    Oh, welcome company."

—May Day Festival Book.

(*The Peasant children appear and lead the* BOY AND GIRL OF TODAY *to the front of the stage where they dress them in gilt paper crowns. During this action the* FAUNS *and* DRYADS *scatter flowers about and move away the hedge disclosing the Maypole with its ribbon streamers.* JUNIPER BERRY *changes the dream May basket for one containing all the things the* BOY *wanted to give the* GIRL, *and the* LEAF BOY *leads the King and Queen of the May to their throne, the seat beside the cottage door. All the Players dance around the Maypole and play such well-known folk games as, "Here We Go Gathering Nuts in May," "On the Bridge of Avignon," "Did You Ever See a Lassie," and "The Chimes of Dunkirk."*)

Runaway Clowns
By Beatrice Creighton

THE PLAYERS

PIERROT—A Little Boy.
PIERETTE—A Little Girl.
As many CLOWNS as you wish.   Twelve is a good number.
Just as many TIGHT-ROPE DANCERS.

RUNAWAY CLOWNS

By Beatrice Creighton

THE COSTUMES

Pierrot and Pierette are dressed after the fashion of old French figures, in white with black trimmings. A child's suit of white pajamas makes an excellent foundation for Pierrot's costume, upon which are stitched or pasted decorations cut from black cambric. Both wear ruffs made of white tarletan. Pierrot may carry a red ukelele, and Pierette an old-fashioned nosegay tied to her wrist.

The clown costume may also be made from a child's sleeping garment, preferably one-piece. Upon this are pasted big circles of red paper. The caps can be made of white crepe paper with red tarletan rosettes. The Clowns wear red bed slippers.

The Tight-Rope Dancers are girls in ballet costume, close-fitting bodices and very full short skirts of tulle or net and ballet slippers.

STAGING

(*The scene is a clearing in a wood. If the play is produced indoors, paint trees on a back drop.* PIERETTE *appears from a clump of trees at left. She looks around, then crosses stage to right and seats herself on tree stump.* PIERROT *follows, as though looking for her, but he shows in pantomime that she is unaware of his presence. He stands directly back of* PIERRETTE *while she sings.*)

PIERETTE (*sings wistfully*):
*Little Pierette cannot forget
 The friend she left behind her;
Little Pierrot, she misses you so!
 Why don't you come and find her?

PIERROT (*eagerly*): Pierette! Do you mean it?

---

*Music for song is "Little Bo-Peep," in J. W. Elliott's "Nursery Rhymes and Songs," published by McLoughlin Bros., Inc., Springfield, Mass.

PIERETTE (*startled*):   Oh! I didn't know you were here.   Why did you follow me?

PIERROT: I will always follow you, Pierette. Please tell me that you meant it.

PIERETTE (*petulantly*): That I meant what?

PIERROT: What you sang, about missing me.   Did you?

PIERETTE: Certainly not!   I never mean what I sing.   Haven't you found that out, Pierrot?

PIERROT (*sadly*):   No.   (*Clasps hands at back, and walks dejectedly several paces.   Turns to* PIERETTE.)   I've only found out how lonesome I am without my play-mate.

PIERETTE: But you said that it was more fun to play alone!

PIERROT: Because *you* said that you were tired of playing with *me*.

PIERETTE: O-oh!   But I was only making believe.

PIERROT   (*sings, to same tune*):
    Little Pierrot could scarcely know
        That you were only playing;
    Little Pierette, I'm so upset (*pantomimes*),
        Still in my heart you are straying.

(*At end of song he takes* PIERETTE's *hands and kisses them.* PIERETTE *smiles, and they make up.*)

PIERETTE: I'm glad you found me, Pierrot. It's quite fearful to be in a strange place all alone. (*Looks around*)   Are you scared, Pierrot?

PIERROT (*sings and pantomimes*):
    Pierette, my dear, we've naught **to fear,**
        There's nothing here alarming.

PIERETTE (*finishes song*):
> Oh, dear Pierrot, you cheer me so,
> I think your bravery charming.

(PIERROT *struts a bit and* PIERETTE *admires him. The more pantomime that can be introduced into this scene, the more attractive it will be. It may end with a dance, at the finish of which* PIERROT *makes a sweeping bow, and* PIERETTE *a low curtsy. There is a noise of talking and laughter off-stage.*)

PIERROT (*obviously startled*): What's that?

PIERETTE: Come, let's hide.

(*They hide behind some small shrubs, as the chorus of* CLOWNS *enters. The* CLOWNS *skip twice about the stage. There are three movements to their opening dance.*)

1. Hands on hips, kick (*four bars of music*). Stop with jump, and clasp hands above heads.

2. Cross feet back and forth, in rhythm, holding hands.

3. Sway back and forth, in rhythm, arms lightly placed on shoulders. End with a solid bow. Clowns *must* all bow together. Music for dance is "The Parade of the Wooden Soldiers."

*Clown Song

> The circus clowns, every one
>> Have run away, you see, you see;
> We're most impertinent, we know,
>> But gay as gay can be.
> The circus life has lots of faults,
> We're tired of turning somersaults!
> For once we'll do just as we like
> We clowns are on a STRIKE!

†Drill

(*Partners facing.*)
> Runaway Clowns,
> Do what they like;

---

*Music for Clown Song is "Jacky Frost" in "Songs for the Little Child," by Clara Belle Baker, published by the Abingdon Press.

†Music: "Peas Porridge Hot."

Work is a bore,
So we all strike!

FIRST CLOWN: Aren't we having fun? I'm ever so glad we ran away!

SECOND CLOWN: Let's sit down and rest awhile. It was a long road to come, all the way from Clown-town.

THIRD CLOWN: Yes, indeed! I ran so fast to keep up with you, I lost my breath.

FIRST CLOWN: I told you not to come. You're much too little to belong to a Strike.

THIRD CLOWN (*ready to cry, for he is the smallest one of all*): I'm not little. I'm big!

FOURTH CLOWN: Well, even big clowns get tired sometimes. Let's all sit down.

(*The* CLOWNS *walk off in two's and three's, and seat themselves on the floor, near the back of the stage.* PIERETTE *and* PIERROT, *in their hiding places, sneeze. They are loud sneezes, easily heard in the audience.*)

SIXTH CLOWN: What's that?

SEVENTH CLOWN: It sounded like a sneeze.

SIXTH CLOWN: It didn't sound like a Clown-sneeze. Some one else is here. Come on, let's hunt.

(*Jumps up, but, before the others follow* PIERROT *and* PIERETTE *come out from the shrubbery.*)

PIERETTE: You needn't hunt. It's just us. We won't hurt you.

EIGHTH CLOWN: Who are you? You don't look like people, and you certainly aren't Clowns.

PIERROT: She's Pierette. (*Points.*)

PIERETTE: He's Pierrot. (*Points.*)

NINTH CLOWN: Pierrot and Pierette! Those are funny names. Where are you going?

PIERROT: We haven't quite decided.

TENTH CLOWN: Would you like to stay here and belong to our Strike? We ran away from the circus, you know.

PIERETTE: Oh, yes, Pierrot, let's stay with these nice creatures and watch them do their tricks.

ELEVENTH CLOWN: We don't do tricks any longer. That's what the Strike's about.

PIERETTE: Oh, I'm so disappointed. I've never in all my life been to a circus.

NINTH CLOWN: Why haven't you ever been to a circus?

PIERROT: They didn't have any where we came from.

TWELFTH CLOWN: Well, of course, it's against what we decided. But we might do one or two tricks as a special favor.

NINTH CLOWN: Yes and our games are very instructive. Would you like to watch us do our daily dozen?

PIERROT AND PIERETTE: Oh, yes! Yes!

NINTH CLOWN (*who must have a clear, carrying voice*): Come on, Clowns!

(*They line up in three rows, and the* NINTH CLOWN *leads the drill.*)

Drill.

Position!
Arms up!
1, 2; 1, 2; 1, 2; 1, 2.
Position!

Arms out!
1, 2; 1, 2; 1, 2; 1, 2.
Position!

Hands on hips!
Bend at knees!
1, 2; 1, 2; 1, 2; 1, 2.
Position!

Salute Mothers!
Salute Fathers!
Salute Everybody!
Rest!   (*They all tumble down.*)

PIERETTE: How splendid! I had no idea that Clowns were so intelligent.

TWELFTH CLOWN: Wait until you see the next trick. It's the best of all.

TENTH CLOWN: I'll get the equipment. It's just outside.

(*He drags in a see-saw board, and as many of the* CLOWNS *as possible pile on.   The others use their arms to represent see-saws and raise and lower them with the music.   Music may be taken from any school music book for the primary grades.   Chorus sings:*)

See-saw, see-saw, up and down we go.
See-saw, see-saw, now we're high and low.
See-saw, see-saw, gayly now we play.
See-saw, see-saw, happy all the day.

(*The Forest gradually darkens as if the afternoon was changing to night.   PIERETTE yawns and stretches out her arms to PIERROT.*)

PIERETTE: I am ever so hungry, dear playmate, and it is growing dark. We shall have to be going home soon.

PIERROT (*looks distressed and runs off-stage for a moment. He returns, holding his hands together as if there were something precious inside*): Here is your supper, dear Pierette;

fresh, crisp moonbeam slices and a bluebell filled
with newly fallen dew.

PIERETTE: Dear Pierrot, thank you! That is
my favorite supper.

(In pantomime she takes the fairy food from PIERROT *and eats
it daintily, sharing it with him. Then the two join hands and
turn to the* CLOWNS, *whose see-sawing has almost stopped as they
watched the pantomime.)*

PIERETTE: Good night, dear Clowns. Thank you
for all your amusing tricks.

PIERROT: Good night, my dear fellows. Good
luck to the Strike, whatever it is.

*(*PIERROT *and* PIERETTE *exit, leaving the* CLOWNS *alone.)*

FIRST CLOWN: They're gone!

SECOND CLOWN: We're alone.

THIRD CLOWN: They've gone home.

FOURTH CLOWN: They had their supper.

FIFTH CLOWN: The Circus is having supper at
this time.

SIXTH CLOWN: We are a long way from home.

SEVENTH CLOWN: We haven't any supper.

EIGHTH CLOWN *(with determination)*: Well, this is a
Strike.

NINTH CLOWN: What good is a Strike, I should
like to know.

TENTH CLOWN: No home. No supper. No light.

ELEVENTH CLOWN: I wonder if they are thinking
about us at the Circus.

TWELFTH CLOWN: Boo-hoo-hoo! *(All cry in chorus.)*
(The stage gradually becomes lighter as if the moon had risen.

Footsteps and excited voices are heard outside. The CLOWNS *hide in dismay. The* TIGHT-ROPE DANCERS *come in carrying small picnic baskets. They appear tired and drop down cross-legged on the stage.*)

FIRST DANCER: The Circus can't go on tonight without them.

SECOND DANCER: Silly, lazy, little Clowns!

THIRD DANCER: They don't deserve their supper.

FOURTH DANCER: But we brought it to them.

FIFTH DANCER: All the long, long way from town!

SIXTH DANCER (*peeping inside her basket*): A thick ham sandwich and a piece of apple pie.

SEVENTH DANCER (*holding her basket high*): A big rosy apple and a bottle of creamy milk.

EIGHTH DANCER: I wish they had not run away. I miss them so.

NINTH DANCER: The Manager is going to advertise for more Clowns in the morning.

TENTH DANCER: But we don't want new Clowns, do we?

ELEVENTH DANCER: That is just what the Manager said. He said that he wanted his dear little old Clowns home again.

TWELFTH DANCER: But they are not here. We shall have to look further.

(*As she finishes speaking the* CLOWNS *rush pell-mell from their hiding places and join the* DANCERS, *sitting down beside them to eat their supper, the* DANCERS *feeding them. When the baskets are empty, they pull out their watches, hidden in their pockets.*)

A Clown: There may be time to get back to the Circus for the evening performance.

A Dancer: Plenty of time!

(In pairs the Clowns *and* Tight-Rope Dancers *dance, then run off the stage, waving their hands gayly to the audience.)*

Hans Who Made the Princess Laugh

By Mary E. Carpenter

THOSE WHO MUST BE IN THE PLAY

THE TWO GUARDS.
A BEGGAR WOMAN.
A KING.
THE SAD PRINCESS.
A COOK.
SOLDIERS.
A POET.
HANS.

THOSE WHO SHOULD BE IN THE PLAY

A MUSICIAN.
A TUMBLER.
A SINGER.
MANY VILLAGERS.
A GARDENER.
A DOG.
FLOWERS.
BIRDS.
ANYONE ELSE YOU CAN THINK OF.

HANS WHO MADE THE PRINCESS LAUGH

By Mary E. Carpenter

THE SCENERY YOU NEED

If you can be out of doors, you may use natural surroundings and just pretend it is the castle garden. If you are indoors, you might take sets of screens and cover them with gray paper, marked with chalk to look like a stone wall. Cardboard, cut in the shape of a turret wall, may be painted and fastened with thumb tacks to the top of the screens. If children do not take the parts of flowers, you must put some make-believe flowers about the stage. You do not really need a curtain, for no one is on the stage when the play begins and every one goes away at the end.

COSTUME SUGGESTIONS

Fairy-tale illustrations furnish appropriate costume suggestions. Long stockings with socks rolled down over them to the ankle look like tights and shoes. Bloomers are full and short. Tunics are long-sleeved, or entirely sleeveless, and worn over tight linings. Sweaters in plain colors serve well as such linings. Helmets, belts, and crowns may be fashioned of cardboard and painted gayly. Needed accessories are: Spears for the guards and soldiers. A sceptre for the king. A handkerchief for the princess. Food and money for Hans. A golden goose for Beggar Woman. A ladle for the cook. A long scroll of poems for the poet. Music for the singer.

MUSICAL SUGGESTIONS

All pantomime acting may be done with or without incidental music. Special dances and drills may be introduced. The smallest children may have a simple dance built on skipping or running for the Flowers' rhythm. The villagers may use any folk dance of European origin, and the soldiers may build a drill on any very old European march. Special characters may use as entertainment for the princess poems and songs learned during the year. Hans' march should really be the "Snail-Shell Game" known in every primary school. It is advisable to select European music rather than American as the fairy-tale

came from that source. Music in the well-known collections
of folk dances and songs furnishes fitting material, and it is
easy to obtain such records for a victrola if a piano is not
obtainable.

THE STORY OF THE PLAY

There was once a very sad princess who never
could be made to smile. At last the king in despair
decreed that he who could make the princess laugh
should not only win her hand but be heir to half the
kingdom as well. Many came before the castle wall
to try their luck, but none could win her. Hans, the
peasant, watched with the other villagers, and was
angry at the treatment given a poor old beggar by
the guards and those who failed. He offered her
what little he had, whereupon she gave him a magic
golden goose, for in truth she was a fairy. Now
when the people saw that marvelous goose they
tried to pluck its feathers, but no sooner had they
touched it or any one holding Hans' goose, than they
found themselves unable to break away. When the
princess saw Hans and his long trail of unwilling
followers, including many who had tried for her
hand, she laughed till the king thought she would
never stop! Of course Hans won the princess.

THE PLAY BEGINS

(Two GUARDS *enter, marching with spears in their right hands.
They make up a long march, ending at opposite corners of the
stage quite near the audience. They stay there until the play is
through, for it is these* GUARDS *who tell the whole story. The* FIRST
GUARD *is very dignified, while the* SECOND GUARD *may be as
funny or stupid as he wishes.*)

FIRST GUARD:
>We have made for you today
>A very simple little play
>Of a princess—

SECOND GUARD: Very sad!

FIRST GUARD: And a little peasant lad.

SECOND GUARD:
> In this castle dwells the maid,
> And her father, old and staid.

FIRST GUARD:
> She's so proud she's never smiled,
> And the king is nearly wild
> Watching his unhappy maid.
> He is very much afraid—

SECOND GUARD:
> She will ever single be,
> So he has made a grave decree.

FIRST GUARD:
> "To him who makes the princess laugh,
> Her hand; and of my wealth, one half!"

(*The* PRINCESS *enters now and stands behind the garden wall. If it is tall, she must stand on a table or chair. She weeps sometimes, is angry with some who try for her hand, and always appears to be very unhappy.*)

SECOND GUARD:
> Here you see the castle wall.

FIRST GUARD:
> And the magic garden gay,
> Where the flowers do their best
> To drive the princess' tears away.

(*The* GARDENER *has been tending the flowers during this last speech. He is sad to see the* PRINCESS *weep. He has an idea. He coaxes the flowers and birds to dance for the* PRINCESS, *but she will not smile.*

The DOG *who is with the* GARDENER *all through the play does all the tricks he can think of.*

The VILLAGERS *come running in and dance or sing for the* PRINCESS, *but they, too, fail to make her smile and feel very sad.*)

HANS *comes in with the* VILLAGERS. *No one knows yet that he
is the hero.*
The BEGGAR WOMAN *also comes in. People push her about.
She is pitiful, old, even lame if she wishes to be.*)

FIRST GUARD:
> How the princess hates a crowd!
> Says dogs shouldn't be allowed.

SECOND GUARD:
> But she can't send us away
> Else there wouldn't be a play.

FIRST GUARD:
> That's quite enough for you to say!
> Here's the king come back from chase.
> Beggar Woman, in your place!

(*The* BUGLER *marches in with great importance, for he heralds
the* KING. *He struts before the* PRINCESS, *who is disgusted with him.*
The KING *enters, mounts wearily to the* PRINCESS' *side, and
beseeches her to choose a* SOLDIER.
The SOLDIERS *now have a real drill with spears or swords, but
the* PRINCESS *sends them all away. They march sadly off or
remain in one corner.*)

FIRST GUARD:
> The soldiers drill and vainly try
> To make her smile.

SECOND GUARD:
> But she will only sigh and sigh
> All the while.

(*A* SINGER *enters and sings to the* PRINCESS. *A* MUSICIAN,
POET, TUMBLER, *anyone else enters. Each displays his talents in
turn before the disdainful* PRINCESS. *Also each must in some
manner be rude to the* BEGGAR WOMAN.
When the last person tries and fails, he pushes the BEGGAR *to the
ground where she lies helpless.*
HANS *now rushes to the old woman, angry at the laughing crowd.
He helps her to her feet, unties his handkerchief-bundle, and gives
her his bread, cheese, and apple. He also gives her coins.*)

FIRST GUARD:
 See that beggar pushed about
 In and out.

SECOND GUARD:
 She's a nuisance in the place
 Without a doubt.

FIRST GUARD:
 Hans says she's hungry, poor and old,
 And she's cold.

SECOND GUARD:
 A tale of goodness like to this
 Has ne'er been told.

(*The* BEGGAR WOMAN *whispers to* HANS *and from under her cloak draws a* GOLDEN GOOSE, *which she gives him.*)

FIRST GUARD:
 "Oh, what a goose," the astonished people cry.

SECOND GUARD: The cook says, "That's a goose that I would buy!"

(*The* COOK *rushes forward and seizes the Goose, but of course* HANS *must pretend that he is held fast by magic to its feathers. The* GARDENER, BUGLER, VILLAGERS, SOLDIERS *and all those who try for the* PRINCESS' *hand in turn, one after the other, add themselves to the line and pretend to pull the one before away.* HANS *parades with his long line of scowling, crying, kicking, furious followers all about the stage.*

The PRINCESS *now laughs in glee and leaves her high place. She comes right up to* HANS *and takes his free hand.*)

FIRST GUARD: But see what silly magic we have here.

SECOND GUARD: The princess leaves her window and draws near.

(*The* BEGGAR WOMAN *comes forward and touches the* GOOSE. *At once the people are free and sulkily draw away from* HANS.

The KING *invites every one into the castle.*

Every one except the GARDENER, GUARDS, *and* DOG *follow* HANS *and the* PRINCESS.)

FIRST GUARD:
   The king invites you to the wedding ball
   Which we shall give within the castle hall.

SECOND GUARD:
   There's no one here with me but you.
   I guess that means the play is through.

FIRST GUARD:
   Had Hans not made the princess smile
   We might have stayed a longer while.
   But here we go, Dog,

SECOND GUARD: Gardener,

FIRST GUARD: All.

SECOND GUARD (*after all are gone, or if there is to be a party at the end of the play, he says*):
   And leave you just the castle wall.
   Come to our feast in yonder hall!

Baucis and Philemon
By Mary E. Carpenter

THE PLAYERS

BAUCIS.
PHILEMON.
MERCURY.
JUPITER.
CROWD OF VILLAGERS: Men, Women and Children.

BAUCIS AND PHILEMON

By MARY E. CARPENTER

THE SCENERY

The front of the rude cottage may be created by using a set of screens covered with unbleached muslin which has been dyed and painted in a soft tone of wood color. The reverse side of the same set of screens may be used for the interior. The muslin used for the interior should be of a lighter tone. Set the screens so that they form interesting angles in the interior.

THE COSTUMES

Stories of Greek myths, well illustrated, will be of great assistance. "The Adventures of Odysseus" and the "Tale of Troy" by Padraic Colum, illustrated by Willy Pogany, would be of particular value. A light flannel, dyed in well-blended colorings, makes splendid Greek costumes, for this fabric readily falls into the draped line of the Greek costume.

THE PROPERTIES

Roughly-built bench.
Bundle of fagots.
Mercury's staff.
Drape for bench (linen).
Beechen bowl.
Rough linen towel.
Basket.
Herbs.
Loaf of bread.
Brightly embroidered cushion.
Roughly hewn table.
Bowls with food for table.
Earthen dishes.
Wooden cups.
Large pitcher.

STORY OF THE PLAY

Once upon a time Jupiter and Mercury visited the land of Phrygia in human form. They walked the roads as travelers, seeking rest and shelter, but found the villagers of Phrygia inhospitable. At last Baucis and Philemon, an aged couple living in a small cottage on a hill above Phrygia, offered the travelers shelter and food, though they were very poor. As Baucis and Philemon shared their humble repast with the weary travelers, they were astonished to see the food replenish itself. Baucis and Philemon soon realized that they had honored their threshold and offered shelter to guests from the company of the gods. As Jupiter and Mercury departed, rested and refreshed, they thanked Baucis and Philemon for their kindness and showed them how they had miraculously changed the wicked village of Phrygia into a mighty lake. In an instant, they transformed the rude cottage of the aged couple into a beautiful temple, and asked that they might grant the wish closest to the hearts of Baucis and Philemon. Legend tells us the aged couple wished to die together, and that at their death the gods transformed them into trees, the oak and the linden, standing side by side on the hill of Phrygia.

THE PLAY
SCENE I

(The first scene takes place in front of a rude cottage. PHILEMON, who is sitting on a bench, is quiet for some time as he watches the sun setting. BAUCIS, who comes from the hut, speaks to PHILEMON as she, too, watches the sun.)

BAUCIS: How swiftly Apollo speeds across the sky and plunges behind the purple hills of Phrygia. His swift steeds stir the sky into a riot of blazing, flaming color!

PHILEMON: With him he takes another day, leaving but the memories of this one in the sky dust where his steeds have galloped.

BAUCIS: Circling the universe Apollo will drive back again, bringing a new day!

(PHILEMON *turns from* BAUCIS *and speaks directly to* APOLLO *in the sky.*)

PHILEMON: How little we know of the fortunes you hold for us, Warrior of the Sky!

BAUCIS: We do know, Philemon, that Apollo has brought fortune, though seemingly little, enough to make us content. We are content, Philemon, though we live in a humble thatched cottage. We seem to be far happier than those who live in the valley below who have far more earthly blessings than we! (PHILEMON *listens attentively to* BAUCIS.) Well-a-day! We are fortunate to live up here on the hilltop, from which we can look down and see the lovely gardens below. Surely there can be no more beautiful and fruitful valley in all the world than the one which stretches between these hills of Phrygia. The fields are flourishing—

PHILEMON (*interrupting* BAUCIS): What you have said is true, Baucis, but—

BAUCIS: Why do you frown? You are sad! Surely not because their soil has yielded forth a rich harvest? Surely not that!

PHILEMON: No—no, not that! But it is very hard to understand why people, blessed as they are with the fruits of earth, should be so wicked, for they are wicked, Baucis.

BAUCIS: That I know. I have heard them quarreling and speaking of one another unfairly.

PHILEMON: More than that, they are so wicked as to make fun of those who are tired and hungry, of strangers traveling through the village. They set their dogs upon those who pass through their streets on foot.

(*A commotion is heard in the distance, children's voices and the barking of dogs.*)

BAUCIS: I have never heard the dogs bark so loudly before! I fear for some stranger even now, Philemon, for the dogs bark cruelly. They snarl and are angry.

(BAUCIS *and* PHILEMON *look down the road and see two strangers approaching.*)

PHILEMON: It is as I have said; there are strangers on the road. Two men are coming in the distance followed by children who mock and laugh at the strangers.

BAUCIS: They are but poorly dressed and look as though they might not have enough to pay for a night's lodging.

PHILEMON: Come, Baucis, let us go and meet the strangers and offer them shelter.

BAUCIS: Our hut is rude but they are welcome to its cover. You go, Philemon, while I hasten to make ready food and drink for them.

(BAUCIS *goes inside the hut. As* PHILEMON *is about to meet the strangers he watches them, followed by a crowd of* VILLAGERS *who mock and shout at the two men. When the* VILLAGERS *see* PHILEMON *step forward to speak to the strangers, they slink away out of sight.*)

PHILEMON: Welcome, strangers, who have walked the long dusty roads this day. Welcome! (*The strangers do not seem to hear* PHILEMON *when he first speaks.*) Welcome, I say, strangers!

MERCURY: These are kind words, indeed, friend.

Your welcome is very different from the one we received in the village.

JUPITER: Being set upon by angry dogs and driven from the streets by stones and ugly words is scarcely what one would call a welcome at all.

(*The two travelers again bow in gratitude and then follow* PHILEMON *into the cottage.*)

SCENE II

(*The second scene is inside the hut. As the guests and* PHILE-MON *enter,* BAUCIS, *who is carrying a bundle of fagots from the shed, places them on the floor and greets their guests.*)

PHILEMON: We are honored to have you cross our humble threshold! We have but little and that is yours.

(BAUCIS *and the guests bow to one another with great dignity.*)

BAUCIS: Here you will not find a mansion with master and servant, but rather a cottage in which Philemon and I, Baucis, Philemon's wife, are all its household—master and servant alike!

MERCURY: Pray tell me, friends, why do you live in such a bad neighborhood?

PHILEMON: Among other reasons, no doubt, that we may welcome you to our hut; and truly you are welcome. We would make you what amends we may for the inhospitality of our neighbors.

JUPITER: Well said, kind Philemon, and if the truth must be told, my companion and I need some amends. Those children—

MERCURY: Those rascals!

JUPITER: Those little rascals, indeed, have be-spattered us finely with their mud-balls.

MERCURY: And one of their curs has torn my

cloak which was ragged enough before their teeth got into it. I struck that dog across his muzzle with my staff so that I think you may have heard him yelp even this far off.

BAUCIS: We heard many a yelp and snarl from the village and felt ashamed for our neighbors, that we did.

(PHILEMON *places a bench for his guests to sit upon and* BAUCIS *covers the bench with a piece of cloth as she asks the guests to sit down.* BAUCIS *next fills a beechen bowl with oil or water that the strangers may wash.*)

BAUCIS: Come, Philemon, while our guests are washing the road dust from their hands, gather some herbs from the garden. I would make our soup more tasty.

PHILEMON: Here they are. (PHILEMON *lifts a basket, in which are herbs, from a peg on the wall.*) They are fresh for I gathered them this noon. (PHILEMON *turns to the strangers.*) Do you know, travelers, in all my whole life I have never been more than a score of miles from this blessed spot?

BAUCIS: This is true, Philemon, and I have dwelt with you from my youth upwards.

PHILEMON: Earning our bread by honest labor,—

BAUCIS: Always poor—but content!

(*While all are merrily talking* BAUCIS *is very busy. She places a brightly embroidered cushion upon the bench where the guests are to sit at table. On looking at the table, she finds that one leg is shorter than the others, so she places a piece of wood under the short leg. Next* BAUCIS *rubs the bare table with sweet smelling herbs which she takes from the herb basket hanging on the wall. No cloth is on the table, but* BAUCIS *sets it with bowls of olives, cornel berries, radishes and cheese. All are served in earthen dishes. Last of all,* BAUCIS *places a pitcher and wooden cups on the table and then asks the guests to sit down.*)

PHILEMON: My good wife, Baucis, makes most excellent cheese!

BAUCIS: It would be well to say little of that until our guests have judged for themselves.

MERCURY: Tell me, friends, was there not a lake, long ago, covering the spot where the village now lies?

PHILEMON: Never in my day, nor in my father's nor my grandfather's. There were always fields and meadows just as there are now, so long as I can remember. And I suppose the fields and meadows always will be there.

JUPITER: I am not so sure of that!

(PHILEMON *and* BAUCIS *wonder at what the stranger has said, yet neither dares to ask him further questions.*)

MERCURY: And now a slice of your brown loaf.

(BAUCIS *cuts a piece of bread from the loaf end.*)

JUPITER: And a little of that honey. It is the color of transparent gold and has the sweetness of a thousand flowers, but of such flowers as never grew in earthly gardens!

MERCURY: I would also have more of this cooling drink. It has been such a hot day—

JUPITER: And we have traveled far!

BAUCIS: I am sorry and ashamed. The truth is, there is hardly another drop in the pitcher!

MERCURY: May I hold the jug? (MERCURY *looks into the jug, then starts to pour milk into his bowl and that of* JUPITER *while* BAUCIS *and* PHILEMON *look on in wonder.*) Why, there is certainly more milk, and it is quite as rich and cool as the first bowlful.

BAUCIS (*almost whispering to* PHILEMON): Did you ever see the like?

PHILEMON: No, I never did, and I rather think you have been walking in a dream. Now if I had poured out the milk I would have known just how much was in the jug! There happened to be a little more in the jug than you thought, that's all.

BAUCIS (*aside*): Oh, Philemon, say what you will— these are very uncommon people.

PHILEMON: Well, well, perhaps they are. They certainly do look as though they had seen better days, and I am heartily glad to see them enjoying such a good supper.

BAUCIS: But see—though they eat of the grapes, the bunches remain as though untouched!

MERCURY: And now, just another cup of this delicious milk, if you please, and I shall have supped better than a prince.

(BAUCIS *starts to take the pitcher but* PHILEMON, *curious to discover whether there was any reality in the marvels, takes it.* PHILEMON *slyly peeps into the pitcher and is fully satisfied that it is empty. Suddenly, however, he perceives a fountain gushing up from the bottom of the pitcher, and filling it to the top. He almost drops the jug from astonishment.*)

PHILEMON: Who are ye, wonder-working strangers? Tell me this, for I must know! How could a fountain of milk get into an old earthen jug?

(MERCURY *points to his staff.*)

MERCURY: Here, it is this staff of mine which is always playing such tricks.

JUPITER: And may the pitcher never be empty for yourselves any more than for the needy way-farer. As for you, Baucis and Philemon, the gods have dined at a board where the milk became an inexhaustible fount of nectar and the brown loaf and honey were ambrosia. Here we have feasted as we banquet at Olympus.

MERCURY: And now we must rest, for we must be on our way before the sun comes into the sky.
(*The stage is darkened as if night were settling down.*)

SCENE III

(*This scene should suggest the roadside a little distance from the hut, the hut being off-stage. As the curtain opens* BAUCIS, PHILEMON *and the two guests are walking down the road in the early morning.*)

PHILEMON: Ah, me, well-a-day! If only our neighbors knew what pleasure it is to welcome the stranger on the road.

BAUCIS: Then they would tie up their dogs and never allow their children to throw stones.

MERCURY: They will not need to tie their dogs.

JUPITER: Nor tell their children not to throw stones.

MERCURY: And tell me, where is this village of which you speak? I do not see anything of it. On which side of us does it lie?

(BAUCIS *and* PHILEMON *turn in the direction of the village and are astonished when they do not see it.*)

BAUCIS: The village—

PHILEMON: There is not even a valley!

BAUCIS: A broad lake has filled the valley from brim to brim!

PHILEMON (*turning to the two travelers*): Tell us, what has become of our neighbors? Do you know?

JUPITER: They are no longer men and women, but have become creatures of the water. There was no beauty and no meaning in lives such as theirs, for they had no love for one another, and no pity in their hearts for those who were needy and weary. Therefore, the lake that was of old in these parts has poured itself forth again, to reflect the sky.

MERCURY: And as we part and take the high roads, kind Baucis and Philemon, request whatever favor you have most at heart.

BAUCIS: Let us live together while we live—

PHILEMON: And die together when we go.

MERCURY: That will be as you have wished. And now look you to your cottage!

(*As* BAUCIS *and* PHILEMON *turn to look at their cottage the two strangers vanish from their sight.*)

PHILEMON: Do you see, Baucis, our rude little hut has vanished and there stands a temple more beautiful than mortal mind could build!

BAUCIS: And do you see, Philemon, how quickly Apollo speeds into the sky, piercing the darkness!

PHILEMON: He has circled the universe and brings a new day, Baucis!

Pan's Birthday Party
By Alice Towle

PLAYERS

PAN.
THE FAIRY.
PAN'S ADOPTED MOTHER.
CAPTAIN HOOK.
TEN PIRATES.
MOTHER GOOSE.
BO-PEEP.
BOY BLUE.
OLD KING COLE.
JACK-BE-NIMBLE.
MARY-MARY-QUITE-CONTRARY.
APRIL SHOWERS.
QUEEN OF THE MAY.
KING OF THE MAY.
TWO YELLOW BUTTERFLIES.
PANSY.
DAFFODIL.
VIOLET.
BLUEBIRD.

PLACE—Woods around Pan's home.

PAN'S BIRTHDAY PARTY

By ALICE TOWLE

COSTUMING

Pan wears a forest costume of green sateen trimmed with brown leaves. A jaunty feather adorns his hat. The fairy is dressed in white, spangled with Christmas-tree tinsel. Pan's mother, this part being taken by the teacher in order to make things run smoothly, wears an old-fashioned print dress, white apron, and little white cap. The pirates and Captain Hook are fierce indeed, in true pirate costume which consists of their regular trousers and shirts with sashes, kerchiefs and bandanas of bright sateen. They wear curtain rings in their ears and handsome homemade boots of oilcloth, topped with scarlet. They carry rubber daggers and have their faces made up to appear ferocious. Mother Goose and her children are dressed to copy pictures in Mother Goose books, Jack-Be-Nimble wearing his nightie. April Showers is dressed in soft gray with crystal spangles. The King of the May is magnificent in purple sateen. His Queen is dressed in pink and is adorned with apple blossoms made of paper. The bluebird and the flower costumes are made of crepe paper, and the yellow butterflies flutter about in tarletan with tarletan wings.

STAGE PROPERTIES

A Maypole trimmed with streamers in pastel shades. A huge birthday cake—made of a cheese box iced by the baker in pink and white, with "Happy Birthday Little Pan" written on the top. Holes are bored in the box before it is iced and in these are slipped Fourth of July sparklers which are lighted before the cake appears.

MUSIC AND POETRY USED

Mendelssohn's "Spring Song" for the fairy dance.
Pirates' Song. Set to "The Brownies" in "Songs of the Child World," Riley and Gaynor, No. 1.
Music for horseshoe orchestra in Arnold Collection of Rhythms, "Little Ensign."

Little Boy Blue, Butterfly, and Pansy, in "Songs for Children," by Dora Buckingham.

Rain Song, Daisies, songs with music in "The Kindergarten Children's Hour."

Little Bo-Peep and Little Boy Blue, in "When We Were Very Young," by A. A. Milne.

Daffodil and Violet, "Songs of the Child World," Riley and Gaynor, No. 1.

Pretty Little Bluebird, "Small Songs for Small Singers," by Neidlinger.

ACT I

(*The curtain rises on a woodland scene.* PAN's *house occupies the center of the stage. It is a tiny house built of large blocks, with windows on either side curtained in yellow, and a wide doorstep on which* PAN *sits dejectedly, one arm thrown about the neck of a large stuffed dog. Whole little birch trees just in leaf make our woods seem most natural, and from these trees as well as from the house hang paper wisteria blooms and real lilacs in all shades of purple. As* PAN *sits forlornly on his doorstep, a little* FAIRY *enters at left and dances gayly about. All at once she discovers* PAN *to her great surprise.*)

FAIRY: Who are you?

PAN: My name is Pan.

FAIRY: Where did you come from?

PAN: Oh, from nowhere in particular.

FAIRY: Why are you so sad?

PAN: Well, you see I have always lived alone in the woods and I've never had a birthday.

FAIRY: Oh, Pan, I'm so sorry, for I've had hundreds of birthdays and they are great fun. I'll see what I can do to help you. (*Waves her wand.*) Pan, Pan, I've thought of something lovely for you. Guess what it is!

PAN: I can't guess.

FAIRY: Well, I'll tell you, I'll bring a mother for you.

PAN: Oh, goody! Will you bring her to my little house? (FAIRY *waves wand and* MOTHER *appears.*)

MOTHER: So this is the little boy I dreamed about last night!

FAIRY: Yes. (PAN *runs up and throws his arms around the mother's neck.*)

PAN: Will you really be my mother?

MOTHER: Yes, dear, if you will be my little boy. You see I've wanted a little boy of my own, but they are hard to find.

PAN: I shall love to have you for my mother.

MOTHER: Now that is settled, tell me what makes you so sad.

PAN: Well, you see, I have always lived here alone in the woods and so I've never had a birthday. I do want one.

MOTHER: Dear me, let me think. . . . Oh, Pan, I have an idea. You can have all your birthdays at once and all the guests you want.

PAN: Can I really? What fun!

FAIRY: Whom will you invite to your birthday party?

PAN: Let me see. Oh, I think I would like the pirates from the Never Never Land.

FAIRY: All right, Pan, I will invite them.

(*Waves her wand and the* PIRATES *march in one by one and group themselves five on either side of* PAN'S *house.* CAPTAIN HOOK, *with his hook displayed, stands in center. They sing.*)

Yo-ho, yo-ho, we are the Pirate Band.
We come from the Never Never Land.

We used to be bad,
But it made us all too sad;
So now we are as good as good can be,
We used to be bad,
But it made us all too sad;
So now we are as good as good can be.

Yo-ho, yo-ho, and I am Captain Hook,
I'm sure that you've read of me in a book.
I did not like Pan,
Oh, I was a wicked man,
Now I'm good and with these others, pirates all,
We have come to make a call,
Yes, have come to make a call,
We've come on little Pan to make a call.

PAN: Thank you, that is very nice. Will you play us a tune now?

PIRATES: Aye, aye, sir.

(MOTHER *gives out horseshoes to* PIRATES, *who keep time to the piano by tapping on them.*)

PAN: You play very well. Will you sit down now?

(PIRATES *all come to right of house and sit down.*)

FAIRY: Now, Pan, whom would you like me to bring next?

PAN: Let me see. Oh, let us invite Mother Goose and some of her children.

FAIRY: Pan, I will call them.

(*She waves her wand and* MOTHER GOOSE *enters, followed by several of her children.*)

MOTHER GOOSE: How do you do, Pan? We are so glad to come to your party. I've brought some extra guests with me. Come, Little Boy Blue.

(*All the Players on stage sing.*)

ALL PLAYERS:
Oh, Little Boy Blue, when you woke, my dear,
Did you blow your horn both loud and clear?
Did the cows come back? Did the sheep come, too?
Little Boy Blue, oh, tell me true,
Of all that happened to you that day
When you went to sleep down in the hay.

LITTLE BOY BLUE: Of course I'll tell you some time, but just now I see Bo-Peep and I have to talk to her.

(LITTLE BOY BLUE *and* BO-PEEP *recite the dialogue embodied in the story poem "Little Bo-Peep and Little Boy Blue" by A. A. Milne, beginning, "What have you done with your sheep, Little Bo-Peep?" This dialogue continues accompanied by appropriate pantomime as the two plan to care for their sheep together, have tea, play with* BOY BLUE'S *horn, and finally be near each other always in the hills.*)

PAN (*clapping his hands*): Oh, I'm so glad they came; are you not glad, too?

ALL: Yes, Pan, we are as glad as can be.

MOTHER GOOSE: I brought little Jack-Be-Nimble with me. Come, Jackie, show Pan what you can do. (*All sing.*)

Jack be nimble, Jack be quick.
Jack jump over the candlestick.

(JACK *jumps over a candlestick.*)

MOTHER: Come, Jackie, and sit over here.

MOTHER GOOSE: Now, Old King Cole, can you sing for us?

OLD KING COLE: Yes I can sing. (*Sings.*)
Old King Cole was a merry old soul
And a merry old soul was he.

He called for his pipe and he called for his bowl
  And he called for his fiddlers three.

PAN: Thank you, Old King Cole.

OLD KING COLE: You are welcome, Pan.

PAN: Mary, Mary, what is your other name?

MARY: Mary-Mary-Quite-Contrary, Pan.

PAN: Well, how does your garden grow?

MARY (*curtsying to* PAN): With silver bells and cockle shells and pretty maids all in a row.

PAN: How pretty! I should like to see it.

MARY: You may, if you will come home with me.

PAN: Oh, Mary, couldn't you bring your garden to my party?

MARY: Pan, wouldn't that be fun? I'll see.

FAIRY: Oh, look who is coming, Pan! The King and Queen of the Woods!

PAN: Dear me, I do hope we have a throne ready.

FAIRY: Right here, Peter.

(*She waves her wand and uncovers a draped chair that serves as a throne.*)

(*All sing.*)

Summer is here. Summer is here.
The snow is all melted; the brooks running clear.
For summer is here, yes, summer is here.

Summer is here. Summer is here.
The violet blossoms; the bobolink's near,
For summer is here, yes, summer is here.

(KING *and* QUEEN *bow low.*)

KING: We have come to your party, little Pan.

QUEEN: And we have a surprise for Mary-Mary-Quite-Contrary. We found her garden looking so sad because she had left it behind that we brought it with us.

PAN (*joyfully*): This is the nicest birthday party in all the world, for everything happens just the way I wish it would. But who is this little gray lady?

(APRIL SHOWERS *enters.*)

KING: That is Miss April Showers. Come, my dear, won't you dance for us?

(KING *and* QUEEN *are seated on throne; butterfly pages stand at back.* APRIL SHOWERS *dances and smiles. As she finishes, everyone sings.*)

To the great brown house, where the flowers live
Came the rain with its tap, tap, tap,
And whispered, "Violet, Pansy, and Rose,
Your pretty eyes you must now unclose
From your long, long, winter's nap,"
Said the rain with its tap, tap, tap.

(FAIRY *goes out and comes running back, chasing a little* BLUE-BIRD.)

FAIRY (*sings*):
Pretty little Bluebird, why do you go?
Come back, come back to me.

BIRD (*sings*):
"I go," said the bird, as he flew on high,
"To see if my color matches the sky."

PAN: But where is Mary's garden?

QUEEN: Oh, Pan, we wrapped the flowers up in seeds and bulbs again to carry with us. So Mary will have to water them before they grow.

(MARY *comes forward and waters little rolled-up seed packets and bulbs. The flower children are ready to enter at the right moment from behind the throne. The first to grow is a pansy.)*

PANSY (*sings*):

When I look at a gay little pansy
I see a face like my own,
With two bright eyes and a queer little nose
And a mouth that could smile if it chose.

PAN: Thank you, Pansy.

(MARY *sprinkles seeds again; this time a daisy grows.*)

DAISY (*sings*)

Little Miss Daisy lives in the grass,
Pretty little flower-lass.
Her cap frills are as white as snow,
She nods a greeting, so, and so.

(MARY *sprinkles another seed; this time a violet grows.*)

VIOLET (*sings*):

Tender little violet, coming in the spring,
Happy hopes of summer to our hearts you bring.
Your delicious perfume, scenting all the air,
Guides us where you're hiding in the woodland fair.

(MARY *touches a bulb; this time a daffodil grows.*)

DAFFODIL (*recites*):

Daffy-Down-Dilly has just come to town
In a petticoat green, and a bright yellow gown,
Daffy-Down-Dilly, just up from her bed
Shaking her flounces and nodding her head.

(BUTTERFLIES *come from behind throne and fly about garden.*)

ALL THE PLAYERS (*sing*):

Oh, butterfly, bright, with your beautiful wings
That are painted the color of lovely things;
So frail and so tender they carry you high.
Way over the blossoms you flutter by!

MOTHER: Now, let us have the birthday feast. Can everyone eat ice cream?

Curtain for Act I

ACT II
The Same as Act I

Kindergarten tables in a long line are covered with white cloths. The Maypole is in the center with ribbons stretched all around the table. In the middle of the table is the birthday cake all sparkling. All the Players grouped around the table sing:

Happy Birthday, Pan,
Little Pan, we love you.
We have had a merry play
In the woods for holiday.
Happy birthday, Pan!
Little Pan, to you.

The rest of the party is most informal. The Players eat ice cream and lady fingers and have a real birthday feast.